The Captive Committee

The Captive Committee

By

Helen Diane Wilcox

ABOUT THE BOOK

Hoping to have a little excitement in their quiet ordinary lives, a few senior citizens, at the urging of a couple of aging swingers, formed a committee to prepare for their long awaited 50th highschool class reunion, expecting to have a whale of a party. But what they got was a lot more than they bargained for.

Joining the Chairpersons, a retired schoolteacher, a minister's wife, the highschool jock, a full time career woman, a former H-Y member, was a disgruntled, angry psychotic and questionable classmate, who managed to infiltrate their group for the sole purpose of destroying this reunion.

This humorous account of the complicated changes that began happening in their everyday lives as events on the committee goes from bad to worse. The bumpy ride changes all of their lives forever.

DEDICATION

To my dear Wil who listened patiently to each new page and encouraged me every step of the way.

PREFACE

The class that graduated from Spinning High School in June 1946 was one of their most exuberant ones. They eagerly awaited each class reunion, held every five years, joining in the revelry with madcap abandon.

Naturally, those that survived until 1995 had reached a pinnacle, looking forward to the prize; to make it to their 50th class reunion in 1996.

The chairperson of the committee, one of their own, diligently kept an ongoing list of the '46 January and June classes up to date for these reunions.

The list of course was dwindling. Classmates left town, moved, remarried, disappeared or died. Altered as it was through the years, it was the most important link for any committee to keep in touch with their classmates.

Now almost fifty years later, the original people who made up those committees, either passed away, as in the case of the former chairperson, or passed on the task.

This Herculean job has fallen on the shoulders of eight people, some of whom had worked at one time or another on past reunions. Each joined the committee for their own reasons, or more likely, because they were talked into it.

They were told there was no reason why this couldn't be the greatest 50th class reunion ever held. The new chairperson felt highly confident, after all, he had the all-important list. What else did they need?

* * * *

THE COMMITTEE

Listed in 1946 Yearbook:Mildred Joanne Fundelich
Library Staff, A Cappella Choir
Debate Team, Tri-Y

Mildred felt abandoned. She had planned to retire age 65, but found herself out of work much sooner.

She taught high-school English from the middle fifties on, fulfilling an early ambition to train young minds to appreciate and use the language correctly. Hating change of any kind, she found it difficult to cope with the ever-changing vocabulary of the times.

Mildred's memory had been on the decline for years and was the reason for her forced retirement at sixty. She had been giving the same assignments over and over to the same students. Most of the kids didn't mind, but an astute parent keeping track of her child's homework did, and turned her in.

As a spinster, she was content with her lot and very devoted to her mother Bella, a widow in her eighties. The children she taught became to her, her ongoing family.

Mildred was not always an easy person to live with and would argue to the exasperation of anyone around if she thought she was right, which was most of the time. But her devotion to her mother, afflicted with Hodgkin's disease, was apparent by the calming influence Bella had on her.

Bella, a small wiry and energetic woman until her illness, had come from Serbia to the U.S. with her family when she was a teen-ager, and her slight accent got more pronounced in times of stress.

The disease left her weak and sometimes unable to walk. But her mind was sharp. She kept Millerd, as she called her, on her toes trying to keep up with her. They shared a keen sense of humor, Bella's cackle always made Mildred laugh.

Often the brunt of Mildred's forgetfulness, Bella found herself stranded at times in places she did not want to be.

1

"Don't forget!" Bella would stress, as Mildred helped her into the bathroom and onto the toilet.

"Of course not, Ma." Mildred would say reassuringly.

"You sure?"

"I promise," said Mildred, even as she walked into her bedroom to gather up her purse and car keys, trying mentally to hold on to the errands she needed to do. "See you Ma!" she'd call out absently, and leave by the back door.

"Millerd? Millerd?... Millllerd!...Bully Sheet!" came the reedy little voice from the bathroom.

Mildred was no longer the robust woman she was in her fifties. At sixty-six her mousy gray hair was permed within an inch of it's life. Plumpness was no longer there to soften her features.

Tight skin made her cheekbones stand out and pushing her glasses up her sharp pointed nose had become a habit. She inherited her mother's close together intense eyes.

Luckily she still had her much needed strength, enabling her to take care of her mother without any help. But her forgetfulness did frighten her, though she tried to ignore it.

Now she had something to look forward to after Dee, her old high-school chum, called her about working on the reunion committee. It should be fun and special, after all the 50th was as special as it could get. She felt honored that Dee remembered her.

The only thing, thought Mildred, that could spoil working on this committee, was that offensive man Gus.

Their first informal meeting had been in a restaurant, and she couldn't remember ever seeing him before. Given her memory, this did not upset her too much. But his foul mouth certainly did.

He used that word. She hated it. Didn't like to read it, didn't like to hear it, ever! It was a scourge on society, and had one of her students so much as whispered it in her classroom, the offender would be marched to the principal's office to be dealt with severely.

Besides, what probably galled her as much or more, was the way he pronounced it.

* * * *

Listed in 1946 yearbook:Maxine (Maxie) Delores Laperi
A Cappella Choir, Girl's Sports Club
Tri-Y

Screw anyone who thought she was too old, Maxie told herself. If she wanted to work another year or two, or even three, that was her business. Besides, she was just given a good raise and that certainly would help down the road in raising her Social Security payments. Along with her retirement plan from the company, she should do all right.

"Too bad there isn't an easier way to get to work," she said out loud. "Commuting's the pits, specially when it's raining."

The dark road glistened ahead of her in the early spring morning. Silhouettes in passing cars failed to arouse her curiosity this morning. Her thoughts were filled with the call she got from Dee last night. Dee couldn't believe she was still working, and she had to go through the whole rigmarole with her.

People didn't understand.

It wasn't like she would starve or anything if she retired now, but she needed the security. Hal, the rat, left her feeling insecure even after all these years, though she tried to give the impression she had everything under control.

People were always surprised that she had raised her four kids alone without any support, after she kicked him out.

"What's the big deal?" she'd tell them. "It's done all the time."

But nobody knew better than her how big. Come to think of it, she was still doing it. Jeezer her grandson, was living with her now, because her daughter Carrie had to move to Chicago for her job.

3

At the time, she remembered, she couldn't say no when Carrie asked. Jeezer had only a year left of high school and didn't want to transfer or leave his band, "The Smokin Zebras."

Having a teen-ager in the house did have it's drawbacks, but what else could she do, she asked herself a hundred times.

But Jeezer? What a name. She was still trying to get used to it. Abiezer Sneed. Carrie was heavy into the Bible when she found the name Abiezer, and Jeezer just sort of evolved.

And he loved it. Said it would be rad when he was famous. She had to admit, she didn't understand any of it, but it's his life and who knew kids?

Checking herself in her rearview mirror she thought, how could I be sixty-six? Course she realized the semi-darkness helped, but the number still surprised her. She knew she didn't feel it, except for maybe the occasional catches here and there. But that's what hot showers were for. I could probably work another ten years, she thought optimistically.

But why, she asked herself did she want to? She had been working all her life it seemed, most of it supporting her family. It had been impossible at times.

Sighing, she focused on the road ahead. "Don't look back," she said softly.

Her free hand moved up through her soft brown curly hair. She knew it would be white if she stopped coloring it. But how could she? It wasn't easy being the oldest woman in the office, and she had to admit, it was getting tougher to keep up with those young minds.

She knew she was damn good at her job, but was she ever that pliable?

If only she'd meet someone. She was tired of being alone and time was definitely running out. I want to be part of a couple, she'd tell herself. Like Buddy and Dee.

The first few years after Hal had been so busy, so full, she didn't have time to give to anyone else. Then she met John, twenty-four years her senior. He was wonderful, he loved her and wanted to marry her.

But he was companionship, someone to have dinner with and go to the races and a movie with. He was not Boris.

She had gone on a double date with Buddy and Dee, before any of them had been married. Boris had been in the Navy with Buddy and she had fallen head over heels in love with him at first sight. Her pulse quickened just thinking of him.

Handsome and tall, he took her breath away. They'd only gone bowling and out for a bite to eat. That was it. She never saw him again until after she was married and pregnant, at Buddy and Dee's wedding.

She kept looking for Boris, or someone like him. Hal at first swept her off her feet and she forgot for awhile, but then Boris again crept into her dreams. Hal could not compete, nor John.

She knew she was a romantic, keeping the faith, but you never know she kept telling herself.

It was only because of Dee that she agreed to be on the committee. With her job and all, she really didn't have any free time, but she and Dee had been best friends in school. "Besides, Dee told her, "it will be such fun, we'll have a ball."

She looked forward to seeing Mildred and Janet again, it had been a long time.

Unable to go to the first get-together, she decided to give this next one a try, since it would be on a Saturday. The thought of one peaceful weekend sounded like bliss. Jeezer's band used the house on Saturdays to practice.

Besides, she'd never seen Buddy and Dee's new home, or them, for some time. It's got to be almost five years since the last reunion. They were still adorable she remembered.

Maxie thought she knew almost everyone Dee mentioned, or heard of them. But she could hardly wait to get a look at this guy Gus. Dee said she couldn't stand him. "He's really strange Maxie," she told her.

A man that Dee couldn't stand? "This I gotta see," she muttered, turning into her reserved parking spot.

* * * *

5

Listed in 1946 yearbook: Leon Jeffry Wadell
Hi-Y and Track

Leon was restless. After all he'd been a salesman all his adult life and needed to be in the thick of things. Working on this committee, was his cup of tea.

Short and round, he still liked to dress in expensive suits, silk shirts, flashy ties and chomp on a good cigar. But thanks to Martha, he had to smoke them outside. She hated cigars.

Since retiring, things had gotten a little slow. A guy could only play so much golf he would complain. And getting together with the boys at the club was getting to be a drag. He was running out of stories and it's hard to be the center of attention without a good story or joke.

Martha had slowed down a lot, practically to a crawl with her arthritis. They couldn't travel like he hoped.

But good old Martha, she had stuck with him, even though she knew he was a bastard. He was sure she knew about the other women, but in her own special way still made him feel like "King of the Hill."

Oh well, that's ancient history now he thought, enjoying the feel of the cigar as he rolled it between his fingers. What with his prostate condition and all, he could no longer fool around, but he had to admit, he missed it. He hated getting old.

"By God, I was really something back then," he liked to tell his cronies, most of them ex-salesmen. "They didn't have all that harassment shit either. Remember? Hell, women knew their place. Guys are scared to take a peek at a gal's tits today, afraid they'll sick the cop's on 'em." he would exclaim, shaking his head in disbelief.

He thought about the women on the committee. They are definitely past their prime, that's for sure. But what the hell, at least they're breathing.

Leon could hardly wait for the first official meeting so he could tell some of his jokes and stories. He smiled at the thought of all the laughter. Being the center of attention was very appealing to him, and he looked forward to a new audience.

Getting the news out about the reunion would be no trouble. After all, he still had a lot of connections and certainly hadn't lost his ability to sell he assured himself, his confidence soaring.

Running his hand vainly through his thick steel gray hair, knowing it was his best feature he frowned, thinking of that first get-together. How the hell did that cue ball Gus get on this committee, he wondered. His friend Buddy only said, "He got in touch with me."

He couldn't remember him from school, and Leon made it a point to know everybody. What the hell was that old fart doing on our committee? That's what he wanted to know.

* * * *

Listed in 1946 yearbook: Daniel (Buddy) Weaver
H-ll Vice President, HI-Y
Block S and Swim Team

Denise (Dee) Gloria Severson
Cheerleader, A Cappella Choir
Tri-Y

They had been high school sweethearts and remembered always as a couple from the 10th grade on. Like Coca-Cola, their names were forever linked.

Dee liked to use her dazzling smile and deep dimples to get whatever she wanted. At fifteen she wore her long blonde hair in a ponytail. Perky and petite and energetic to the point of frenzy, she naturally became a popular cheerleader. The envy of girls, but the boys wanted to cuddle and protect her.

She chose Buddy. Always smiling and eager to please, they made a popular and adorable couple. Buddy wore his thick brown hair in a pompadour to add to his slim barely five foot three frame.

Like other boys in 1945 and '46 who were turning eighteen, they were still eligible for the draft, even though the war was over.

Buddy's first choice had been the Marines, but was turned down because he was too short, so he joined the Navy, much to the delight of Dee.

She loved the way Buddy looked in his tight navy uniform. The way he wore his little squared off white hat jauntily at an angle, behind his pompadour. And always the spare cigarette tucked behind one ear, an attitude he wore with pride.

Buddy carried the small graduation picture of Dee, proudly showing it off to his mates who invariably whistled, thinking Buddy very lucky indeed.

At home in her room, Dee pined and mooned over Buddy's picture. She kissed the black and white photo so often, his smiling lips had a permanent pink cast to them.

Even though it was once again peace time, Dee worried that he would be shipped out and gone for long months at a time.

The closest Buddy got to being shipped out was to San Diego, working in a small navy office, stamping numbers on pages.

Now, forty-nine years later, they scurried after youth and youthful things. Refusing to grow old, they pursued anything that would keep them forever young; vitamins, low fat and healthy foods, and a faithful exercise regime.

Gone was Buddy's pompadour, along with most of his hair, replaced by an expensive thick, brown toupee. Buddy could have well afforded a hair transplant, "But that took too much time," he complained to Dee who was on his case to do it. She knew he avoided it because it might be painful, and Buddy was a real baby about pain.

Dee kept herself fit through aerobics classes, going three times a week. Her hair, much shorter and platinum blonde was maintained by constant visits to her hairdresser. She was rarely without her backless high heels and trendy youthful outfits.

Buddy and Dee had a chain of hardware stores known as, "BeeDee's," managed well by an excellent younger assistant. Being semi-retired, they loved the idea of being in charge of the prize, their 50th class reunion.

Having gone to all of them and sometimes even working on a committee was one thing, but now they would be able to do things their way. They had found fault with so many things in the past, now this reunion would be perfect. Of that, they had no doubt.

They gloated over how much younger they thought they looked than most of their classmates. Neither one would wear glasses, except for reading. Even then, they avoided getting too close to each other with them on.

Dee was glad Maxie was going to join them. They had been best friends in school, and having Mildred and Janet there too, she felt would give her an edge. After all, they always deferred to her wishes in school, and she was counting on it again. "My God," she said to Buddy over their morning coffee. "It's hard to imagine that Millie and Janet graduated with us. "I don't look as old as them, do I hon?" She eyed him, watching for any sign of hesitation.

"Gosh no, you haven't changed," he answered quickly, hearing her need for assurance. "You're still the same sweet, gorgeous adorable girl I fell in love with in the 10th grade."

She dimpled with pleasure, reaching over to pat his hand. "Leon has sure gotten fat, hasn't he?" she asked.

Buddy nodded absently. "What about that old buzzard Gus?" He looked up from the paper. He hadn't meant to bring Gus up, but he had been on his mind since that first get-together, and it slipped out. He tried to act nonchalant.

"Wonder why he wants to work on this committee?" she asked, shuddering dramatically. "He's horrible, Buddy. All he does is look with buggy eyes and swear. And the way he says that word, that's really strange, don't you think?"

She looked at Buddy closely. "How did you say he got word of this?"

Looking down at his paper, Buddy squirmed under her gaze.

"I told you hon, he called."

"But how did he"...she persisted. "I never saw him before, so how did he know we were getting a committee together, that's what I don't understand."

"Beat's me!" he answered, digging his nose deeper into the paper.

"Well, can't we get rid of him?" she demanded. "He's trouble."

"Who's gonna tell him he can't be on the committee?" he asked defensively. "Heck, he looks like he could wipe us all out if he wanted to." He gave her a pitying look. "None of us guys could stand up to him." He paused, "well maybe Jake, if he decides to join us."

He smiled reassuringly at her. "I got it...we'll just ignore the guy!"

* * * *

Listed in 1946 yearbook:Janet Lorraine Carter
A Cappella Choir, Girl's Sports
Club and Tri-Y

Janet lived her life slightly off kilter. She tried to convince herself for a long time that her home life wasn't too bad, but everything had become routine.

Most of the time she wasn't sure where she was since her heavy schedule kept her going at top speed; church committees, women's league, socials. Being the wife of a Lutheran minister was very demanding.

She was a wonderful cook and an avid gardener. Her short white wavy hair stood out against the tan she wore most of the time.

Devoid of any vanity, and with low self-esteem, thanks to her husband, she went about her tasks without complaint. Her slightly plump figure had turned into a comfortable friend, since her husband no longer desired her.

Andrew, her husband of over forty-five years, only talked to her now to inform her of what her day would consist of.

He always had a schedule for her to follow. "The Godman," as she referred to him in her thoughts, knew how to push her buttons, making her feel inadequate, anytime, anywhere.

She didn't really care about being on Dee's committee at first. She only wanted an excuse to be away from the Godman and church duties for a few hours.

But there was another compelling reason. They would probably serve wine, and wine helped her cope.

She could probably get a ride with Millie or Maxie, so if she happened to be coping real good, at least she wouldn't be endangering anyone's life.

Andrew had questioned the purpose of the meetings. "After all," he told her, "I certainly hope our important projects won't suffer or be ignored." She understood perfectly. The church, his projects, always his projects.

A tiny anger started to grow inside her, and for one of the few times in their lives together, she defied him.

"There's no reason to worry. This is something I wish to do outside of the church." She faced his stony gaze, noticing the smirk that crossed his face when she added, "It's important to me Andrew," made her stiffen with resentment.

He shrugged and walked away as if to show her that what was important to her, was simply not important.

That's when she decided she really did want to go. She could do it all. There was always something ready to pop into the oven or microwave, and Andrew would have no reason to complain, since he insisted on a full meal every evening.

She knew this committee would be a whole lot different from the ones she usually shared with the women of the church, most of whom she found to be self-righteous, complaining and hypercritical.

A personal problem did concern her. In her own home, where most of the church meetings were usually held, she could easily excuse herself on the pretext of doing something in the kitchen. But away from home, she had to constantly look for a bathroom.

Her problem was getting worse. She constantly worried about leaving drops or even a puddle in her wake.

After the first get-together she was more than willing to put up with any inconvenience, however embarrassing. It was Gus, he excited her.

He was crude and profane, but she found him utterly fascinating. She knew it was a sin to use the Lord's name in vain, and of course she'd never do it. Somehow though, it gave her a delicious sacrilegious feeling, listening to it. To Gus.

The feeling he stirred in her frightened her, but not enough to keep her from looking forward to the next meeting.

* * * *

Listed in the 1946 yearbook:Jackson (Jake) Everett Hall
Editor, School Newspaper
(Off the Top) Block S
Swim and Gymnastics Team

Jake had been a widower for almost three years. His friends were after him to get out and do things, but until Buddy called him about the committee, he hadn't been ready.

For such a long time he had been lost, going through the motions, getting through the days. His sons were there for him but his despair over losing his beloved Franny made him want to lash out, especially at his sons.

They never gave up on him, and this last year became a little easier. He tried to keep the house up like Franny had. The garden, though neglected, would be starting to bloom soon.

Fran loved the spring, and for the first time in a long time, the spring breezes stirred him into action. He decided to give the garden the attention it needed. Now, after some backbreaking work, it was almost back to the way it was.

Everyplace he looked, he thought of his wife with loving remembrances. Wispy white hair surrounded a lined face. Worry over Fran almost defeated him. His strong six-foot frame became stoop shouldered, the twinkle had gone out of his once smiling blue eyes.

Buddy reminded him that they needed a printer, and even though he was retired, he supposed he could go back to the shop to help the committee out.

He was getting more comfortable with his single life and surprising himself how adept he was getting at things, like cooking and shopping.

He found he was neat because he wanted to be, remembering how Fran always had to tell him to pick up his clothes or put his shoes away. He chuckled, I must have been a real pain in the ass, he thought.

As time passed, calmness began pushing despair out. Not too many things upset him, until he attended the first gathering of the new committee. Until Gus.

He tried to ignore Gus's profanity but wasn't sure he would be able to ignore Gus. He was dumbfounded at Gus's lack of regard for anyone around him.

He didn't look like anybody he knew and he sure didn't fit in, but there was something about him. It nagged at Jake.

Maybe I won't stay on the committee, he told himself. Maybe I'll just do their printing.

When Buddy called to let him know the date of the next meeting, Jake became hesitant. But the heavy guilt trip Buddy laid on him about the printing and probably with a bit of curiosity mixed in, Jake decided to give it one more try, just to see.

* * * *

Listing in the 1946 yearbook: None for Gus Randolf

He knew he was not understood. Good, he preferred it that way, for now. Gus was sure he was smarter than all of them, and told himself he had as much right to be on the fee-ucking committee, as anyone else. They owed him, and he planned to stay! Buddy and Leon, all they could see was the nose on their faces, he could see so much more. His dark eyes narrowed as his thoughts bumped into each other.

13

He slowly rubbed his thick fingers back and forth, feeling the stubble on his large shaved head. A gesture some found to be quite menacing.

The committee, nothing but piss-ants, but he could handle them, he told himself. But Jake on the other hand, might be a problem. He felt it, the surge, the questioning look he got from Jake. Jake thinks he knows something, Gus thought, sure he could read people's minds.

Mostly it came from the looks he got. His neck was thick and corded. His once broad shoulders were slipping into blubber, along with the rest of 5'9" frame. With his overlarge head and dark hooded eyes, it wasn't too hard to read repulsion on people's faces.

Gus had gotten stuck in a time warp in the year 1963. When President Kennedy was assassinated on November 22nd, something snapped in his brain. He knew it was 1995, but could only assimilate to 1963.

That was the beginning of the end of his marriage. His wife could no longer tolerate his fits of anger and paranoia. He was no longer the man she married.

At first, when he would go to his study and write numbers over and over, she accepted it as eccentricity. But she began to find numbers on everything. He even spoke in numbers occasionally.

There had been no children, and Gus did not miss his wife after she left. He preferred his solitude, his numbers. There was so much to do.

He loved numbers, his numbers. Thinking he was being very clever, he used his beloved numbers to convey his thoughts. He even tried sending out letters to a few people, using mostly numbers, but no one answered him. Instead, one of the letters was turned over to the police, who notified the post office.

Postal Inspectors swooped down on him asking a lot of questions. He told them he was a scientist doing an experiment. They told him, fooling with the U.S. Postal Service was extremely dangerous, and let him off with a grave warning.

He changed his residence and no longer put a return address on any mail sent out. And, he made sure not to let the numbers slip out in his conversation.

Special secret numbers became his swear words, used only when he was alone, or muttered quietly to himself.

He would type them on envelopes along with the address, crossing out certain letters, designed to confuse any government official.

He thought his envelopes a work of art, and always managed to type 11.22.63, (Kennedy's death) somewhere on it. Sometimes he typed 63.22.11, just to confuse.

The number eleven, for piss-ant, was usually found after someone's name, along with the number 9525 for fuck, or fee-uck, as he preferred to pronounce it. A special favorite of his.

He liked to spread it out, to prolong it, knowing it irritated people, especially that prissy school teacher.

He enjoyed watching her mouth turn into that thin line of disapproval. She reminded him of his sister Brenda, and he hated Brenda's guts. He planned to use it often at the meetings.

Before he turned his attention to numbers, he had invented a bulletproof helmet. He was absolutely convinced that had President Kennedy been wearing it, he would have survived.

Gus tried several times to see someone in the FBI to show his helmet to.

The week before the Dallas trip he did manage to see an agent. But before he was turned away, he was treated to insults by several more agents. "No way was the President of the United States going to wear a stupid thing like this!" they said holding it up to ridicule.

"What, are you nuts?" and "Get lost!" almost throwing the helmet in his face. Laughter followed him out the door. "Ninety-five, twenty-five them!" he muttered to himself. Any inventions became a private thing after that.

He had been waiting for the 50th reunion, becoming obsessed with the notion and the number. Great number, 50...and great for payback time, he would repeat over and over.

Those ninety-five, twenty-fiving, eleven's had no idea. They needed watching.

THE MEETING: April 22, 1995

"Okay you guys," Buddy said loudly looking around the room, "can we get the meeting started?" Shouting always made his voice an unbecoming falsetto. He once heard himself on tape, and it was humiliating. Touching his toupee with nervous fingers, he wished desperately for a mirror to see if it was the least bit crooked. Heavy sweating was his other problem.

He looked in his wife's direction, hoping to get her attention. She was his mirror.

Unfortunately Dee was busy talking to Maxie, their heads close together. Dee's earrings, large white plastic flowers, swinging on two-inch chains, just missed Maxie's nose.

Buddy began to sweat.

Having Dee's face with her platinum blond hair and heavy make-up that close to her was daunting enough, but to Maxie, the sweet cloying perfume was about to knock her out cold. She must have rolled in the stuff, she thought, trying not to gasp.

Weaving back and forth, Maxie noticed Buddy looking helplessly at Dee. "I think he's trying to get you're attention Dee," she said pointing at Buddy.

Dee turned, dimpling prettily, to give all her attention to her husband. She could hardly contain her excitement. This is going to be so much fun she thought, especially now that her and Buddy will be able to do things their way, something they couldn't do while working on Harriet's old committee.

She had talked Buddy into chairing the committee, now that it was rudderless. Too bad about poor old Harriet, getting sick and dying like that, but at least she lasted long enough to turn over the list to her and Buddy. Dee let out a big sigh, thinking how close they came to not getting it.

Meeting at their house seemed ideal. The location was handy for all of them and the rooms large enough to accommodate almost any size gathering. They had the house built right after they made their first million.

Dee was very proud of the sign on their front porch that read: "HAPPY HAVEN," and the doorbell that played, "Oh What a Beautiful Morning." Naming everything was Dee's idea and Buddy, proudly went along with it.

Dee had decided to use the front room, a place she was particularly fond of, and anxious to show off.

As was Dee's wont, she named it "The Formal Room."

The walls were painted stark white. Each chair and sofa, delicate period pieces on spindly legs, were upholstered in white damask. Elaborately draped white silk lampshades, dripping elongated crystals, perched over tall lava lamps. White globules floated inside the glass, undulating as if to some exotic tune as they sat on polished white end tables.

One had to look closely to see the humorous white pig-shaped coasters, placed discreetly on their surface. Even the glistening white grand piano couldn't hold it's own, and blended quietly into the wall of white drapes behind it. Pictures looked as if they were carved out of uncolored plaster.

The only relief, if you could call it that, was the excruciatingly bright lime green carpeting, with nickel size orange and purple polka dots.

Maxie felt a bit nauseous and tried to keep her eyes averted from the lava lamps and carpeting. Not an easy task. Focusing instead, on the large picture window that offered budding trees stirring gently in the spring breeze. She sighed, thinking how lucky they were to be outside. Dee's perfume wasn't the only thing starting to give her a pain over her left eye.

Checking everything out, her eyes darting here and there, Mildred could hardly wait to get home and tell Ma about this set-up. Ma wasn't great with colors, but this would get a laugh out of her for sure. She took notes.

They gotta be kidding, thought Leon. He and Buddy had been good friends in school, but now only saw each other at the class reunions. He knew Buddy and Dee had done very well with their hardware stores and made a lot of money, but Jeez, he thought, looking around, is this the best they could do?

He started to shake his head in disbelief when he first sat down and looked around, but caught himself, darting a quick look here and there to see if anyone caught it. Only Maxie seemed to notice, but quickly looked away, a slight smile on her lips.

Janet slowly sipped her wine wondering where the bathroom was, and if she should look for it now, or wait awhile. She had come with Maxie and Mildred in Maxie's car and it had been a rather long ride. With her problem, she was sorry now she didn't check it out right away, hoping and praying she wasn't ruining anything. Even with all the precautions, she could never be too sure.

"Holy Shit!" Now ain't this something!" exclaimed Gus, deliberately waiting until after Buddy's start. He looked around. "Whoa-ee, looks like a fee-ucking whore house!"

Expecting only praise for her decor, Dee let out a loud gasp and was momentarily struck dumb.

Mildred fussed on her white on white chair. She fumed at the use of that word. Then rigid with indignation she slid her glasses back up her sharp nose and clamped her lips together, after exclaiming, "Well!"

Leon, taking his first sip of wine gulped, choked and started to cough.

Deciding she had better look for that bathroom after all, Janet got up and no one seemed to notice.

"Buddeeee!" shrieked Dee, getting her voice back. "Buddy do something!" she demanded shrilly.

Buddy could feel the heat radiate under his toupee, knowing he'd have to do something about Gus. Buddy, slight of stature, shuddered at the thought of any altercation, especially with "Sluggo". When Gus approached him about being on the committee he had no idea who he was, but Gus seemed to know him. He didn't seem as scary then, but something had certainly changed.

"Shit," he said under his breath as he faced Gus. "Now you know Gus, that really wasn't very nice, I think you should apologize to my wife here," he pointed in Dee's direction. "She's worked real hard making our home beautiful for us."

Heart pounding, he looked hopefully at Gus, who stared back at him with dark eyes that seemed to Buddy, full of hatred.

"Great," muttered Leon after his choking subsided. I didn't sign up for this shit, he told himself. I hope no one expects me to roust that old fart, I have to watch my prostate.

Sitting off in a corner taking the whole thing in, Jake was thinking to himself, big mistake, I'm not ready for this. After Buddy's call he began to think maybe he really should get out and start living again, but was this the way to start?

Enjoying all the glares he was getting, Gus decided it wasn't time yet. "Oh, okay." He looked at Dee. "I been in some great whore houses, almost as classy...just never seen so much fee-ucking white before. Sorry," he leered.

Intolerable, he's intolerable, thought Mildred, seething unable to even look in his direction.

"Okay...okay honey?" Buddy asked Dee. He gave her a pleading look and silently prayed she wouldn't expect him to do anymore, Jesus that guy was big as a house.

Dee couldn't trust her voice and just nodded her head, she'd let it pass for now, wanting the meeting to continue. But how dare he, she seethed. That Gus better watch out!

Maxie cleared her throat a couple of times, covering up she hoped, the laughter ready to explode within her. She really wanted to laugh, praying, God, please don't let me, even pinching her arm hoping the pain would take her mind off it.

As much as she disliked that awful man, whoever he was, he sure hit the nail on the head. She pinched herself again.

Jake was watching Maxie. His blue eyes brightened, noticing the color fill her cheeks, and how she was trying not to laugh. He noticed a few other things about her too.

Lost in pleasant reverie, he didn't realize Buddy was talking to him until he heard "Jake? Jake?"

"Huh?...what?" he answered turning to the voice. Buddy was staring at him, a pained expression on his face.

Feeling their lack of attention, anxiety gripped Buddy. He could feel his shirt sticking to his back and sweat poring under his arms, under his toupee. The sides of his face were wet. This meeting wasn't going anything like he imagined.

He wanted to duck behind the white couch and smell his armpits to see if his deodorant was still working. The thought of physically offending anyone, was more than he could bear.

Now he had lost control, all because of that shit Gus.

Feeling the silent stares, he tried to remember where he left off. "Oh yes," he continued, stalling to regain some of his dwindling composure· "Can you handle whatever we need to have printed Jake?" He felt shrunken, smaller than his five-three frame·

"Oh sure, my son Billy will let me in the back door of the shop·" He paused. "I know the password."

Relieved, everyone laughed. ·Except Gus. He didn't think it was funny. Ninety-five, twenty-five, he said to himself.

"Okay!" A grinning Buddy said. He stopped shrinking. "Dee said she would be treasurer. Now, who wants to do decorations?" he asked looking down at his list of things to do.

At the moment he looked back up, Janet, having just returned to her seat was raising her glass to her lips. Noticing the movement and forgetting he was not at an auction said, "Great, Janet's got it. Thanks, I'm sure you'll do an outstanding job." Everyone else he noticed, were sitting like slugs. Unperturbed, Janet replied, "No problem·" She was used to being called upon, after all, she was a minister's wife. She got up and went to the bathroom again as soon as Buddy started talking to Mildred.

"How about you helping Jake get the program out?" Buddy smiled. "It has to be special you know, 50 years special and you're just the gal to do it." Buddy was beaming at her and at his own brilliance. He knew he was putting it on pretty thick.

"Why, I think that would be fun," said Mildred forgetting about Gus. She leaned forward in her seat getting enthused and already filling with ideas. "I do have my mother to look after, but I still have plenty of time." She tried to fluff her hair but it was so tightly permed it just didn't fluff. Turning to Jake she asked, "Is that alright with you Jake?"

"Great Mil." Jake hoped it sounded sincere. He wasn't even sure he was going to stay with this group, but he did notice he was having a hard time keeping his eyes off Maxie's legs. They were long and shapely, hmmmm..there was even a bit of thigh.

Gus's unwelcome voice broke in. "I want to mail out all the invitations." Visualizing all those addresses, those numbers, he could hardly contain his excitement, though one would ever know to look at him.

Buddy gave him a long look, wishing he would just go away. "You sure you can handle it? It's a lot of work, and really important." He forgot whom he was talking to.

Gus shot halfway out of his chair, almost tipping it over. "What do you mean, can I handle it?" he growled, thrusting his large glistening shaved head forward.

Buddy paled. Wetness poured from his armpits.

"I'm great with numbers, you'll see. You'll all be surprised at the job I'll do." Gus sat back, waiting.

Dee had hoped that her and Maxie would work on the list together. She had already mentioned it to Buddy, and he agreed. Glaring at him, she waited for him to keep his promise.

Buddy didn't miss the accusing eyes of his wife boring into him. Jesus, he thought, there won't be any living with her if she doesn't get her way. But Gus was the more immediate threat.

"Well," he began lamely. "If there are no objections from anyone, I guess Gus can do it. After all," he tried to lighten the situation with a little laugh, "he was some kind of an engineer, I believe." He kept his eyes averted from Dee but could feel her anger all the way across the room.

Taking advantage of the moment, Gus sneered, "Why should there be any fee-ucking objections? You didn't ask if there were any objections about the school teacher, and what's her name, the one who keeps going to the can." He deliberately pointed to Janet returning to the room for the third time.

"Seeing her embarrassment, Leon felt sorry for Janet. "You bastard," he muttered.

Janet hated undue attention to her problem, and was surprised by his mean remark. It was unnecessary. But she couldn't help herself. Never having met anyone quite like him, she was totally fascinated. Living the kind of life she had, she knew she was certainly sheltered from any such language on her other committees. The Godman would have a stroke if he knew what she was listening to. She almost giggled.

Mildred took greater offense at Gus's remark. Her cheekbones and sharp nose became bright red. Again, disapproval made her thin lips disappear, elating Gus.

Buddy was getting tired. Otherwise he might have thought twice before he did what he did. He looked down at the manila folder he was holding. Defeated, he held it out to Gus.

"Okay, okay Gus. Here's the list." He felt like throwing it in his face, the smug shit, but didn't have that kind of energy left.

Gus's smile was anything but charming as he took the folder. "Thanks Buddy, you all will just love the job I'll do."

Buddy turned away from Gus disgusted. "Leon," he said, needing to see a friendly face. "We talked about you doing the publicity at that first get-together...in that restaurant, do you remember?" he rambled on.

"Yeah, sure I do. I can do that, no problem," Leon said in his kindest tone. He'd show that jerk Gus how to get along. He thought maybe it was time for one of his stories or jokes, but looking around at the glum faces, he wasn't sure if it was proper.

What the hell had he gotten himself into he wondered. Where was all the fun and good times they were supposed to have and just where in the hell did his friend Buddy find this guy, Leon wondered, and why was he here?

"I'll get the message out to the papers and media," he said. "What about the date, I think that's our first priority."

"Sometime in September or October?" offered Maxie.

"Sounds good," Leon agreed.

"Okay," said Buddy, thinking he was finally on a roll. "Everyone agree?"

He looked around, everyone nodded their heads. "Gus what about you?" Buddy asked, surprising himself.

23

Gus smiled. Good, he wanted to be asked. They had better deal with him. "Sounds good," he said nicely. He saw the surprise on their faces. Good, keep them guessing.

Buddy was scanning a two-year calendar. "This is April, so figure we've got about eighteen months till the reunion." He flipped the pages. "Let's see..we've got the 7th, 14th, 21st and the 28th in September, no wait a minute, the 14th is Rosh Hashanah. That's out."

They were looking at Buddy and didn't notice the glaze that came over Gus's dark eyes, or the peaceful look on his relaxed face. The numbers, Gus could feel his skin tingle.

"What about October?" Mildred wanted to know.

Buddy stole a glance at Dee and quickly looked away. If looks could kill, I'd be lying in a heap he thought.

Buddy flipped the page. "The 5th, 12th, 19th and 26th."

Gus' eyes close in bliss.

Janet rested her wineglass on the table, letting out a small giggle at the sight of the coaster. She adjusted the glass so that it covered the pig's snout and eyes leaving the exaggerated belly and curly tail.

When she looked up Gus was staring at her. She felt a hot flush on her face and looked down quickly. Making a grab for her wineglass she knocked it over. "Oh no, why didn't I have the white wine?" she asked watching the white table take on some color for the first time. What's her Ninety-five, Twenty-fiving problem, Gus asked himself disinterestedly.

Dee immediately went into action, and rushed towards the unthinkable. "I'll get something," she said crossly.

Making feeble attempts to stem the flow, Janet became more flustered than ever and began using her hand until Maxie handed her a couple of tissues.

"Oh dear, oh dear!" she kept repeating as the soft absorbent tissue sucked up the red menace. "We should have had this meeting in the garage, but that's probably called the something untouchable, too!" She was babbling and couldn't stop.

Maxie and Mildred got up and tried to help. "Take it easy Janet, it's just a spilled drink. It's not the end of the world."

"Did you see her face? You didn't see her face," she whispered to Maxie.

Before Maxie had a chance to answer, Dee was back with a handful of cloths. "Did any get on the carpet?" she demanded, while making exaggerated swipes at everything.

Janet wanted to throw herself on Dee's mercy, but felt a slight trickle running down her leg. She ran from the room.

Who the hell would ever see it on this rug? Leon asked himself.

Jake missed Franny, she would never have made a fuss like this, over things. Not his beloved wife, never, never. She would have laughed it off saying, "Life's too short to worry about little accidents." As always, he felt the emptiness deep in his chest at the mere thought of her.

Buddy had come over to see if he could help. "It's okay hon." He felt embarrassed by Dee's actions. "Everything looks great." He tried to ignore the pink stain on top of the table. "Come on Dee, it's just an accident," he whispered to her.

"Yes of course," she sniffed, glaring at him. Carrying the dampened cloths out of the room, knowing every eye was on her, she stomped silently on the lime green rug in her size four backless high heels.

Buddy's breath came out long and hard wondering when's this day going to end. "Okay," he said consulting his notes. "I've made a list of different restaurants and hotels. We'll have to check them out and see what dates are available." He looked up indifferently. "Now who wants to go with me?"

Walking back into the room, Dee, all smiles now, raised her hand as did Leon, Mildred and Jake. Buddy grinned.

"We should go as soon as possible, like next week," Buddy suggested, noting the group of hands. "How about Tuesday?"

"Sorry people, that let's me out," said Maxie. "I'd love to go with you, but I have to work." She looked around. "I think there should be enough of you."

Jake turned to look at her, surprised that she was still working. Maybe that's why she looks so all together, he thought.

Maxie caught the look of surprise on Jake's face. She was used to it, but still a little defensive on the subject. What's the big deal...I'm only sixty-six, she'd tell herself.

She supposed everyone here was retired, and good for them if they didn't have to work. She always got that out of place feeling around retirees and somewhat resented it.

One of these days, and she wasn't quite counting them yet, but hopefully she'd be off on a long cruise.

"That's okay, Maxie. We understand." Buddy turned to Janet coming hesitantly back into the room.

She felt the eyes turned towards her and wished a hole would open under her feet.

"What about you Janet?" Buddy asked.

She had heard something about Tuesday. "Oh, ah, Tuesday. Let's see, Tuesday. Oh that's right, I've got Bible study on Tuesday. Sorry." She looked down for her wineglass, but it was gone. Pushing a strand of wavy hair back off her face, she carefully sat down.

All eyes shifted to Gus sitting like a big lump on the dainty chair, overpowering it.

Relishing the pressure he was putting on Buddy, he cleared his throat. "I'm gonna be busy on Tuesday. You all will just have to get along without me." He worked in Texas once where he picked up the drawl, using it when it suited him.

Relief filled the room. Except for Janet. She felt a disappointment she could not understand.

Buddy smiled broadly. "How about ten o'clock Tuesday morning. I've got a large van we can all fit in. We can meet at the park around the corner...okay?"

AFTER THE MEETING

Jake waited for Maxie outside by his car. He knew she was saying her good-byes and he wanted to say something to her. He didn't quite know what, but ... there she was. He felt a stirring in his chest.

He noticed she was fairly tall, around five-six or seven maybe, more in the low heels she was wearing. Nice figure, slim, but he noticed that before, when she got up to help Janet. He liked that too, and her hair looked soft, a pretty brown color. He wondered if it was naturally curly, never giving it a thought that it might really be gray.

Reaching into her purse and rummaging around for her keys, Maxie became aware of Jake walking towards her. He seemed a little stooped. She stopped, noticing over Jake's shoulder Mildred and Janet waiting by her car.

"Hi," Jake said. "I was going to offer you a ride, but now I see you have your car keys, so that must mean you drove," he finished lamely, feeling like a complete ass.

"Yes, I did drive this time, but thanks anyway for asking." Noting his embarrassment she said, "What did you think of the meeting?"

"I certainly hope they're not all going to be like that." He looked around like a conspirator. "Is it just me?"

She liked his eyes, they actually twinkled, and they were the prettiest sparkly blue, surrounded by soft folds of skin.

Maxie leaned closer. "What?"

"Is that guy Gus nuts or what?"

"Both," she laughed, "and a little scary, too."

"That's for sure! "He felt himself warming to the conversation and to Maxie.

"I'd better get to the car," she smiled. "The girls are waiting for me."

Great smile, he noticed. Trying not to show his disappointment, Jake gave her a slight bow. "Well, I guess I'll see you next time." He grinned, realizing he was finally committing to something.

"Right, bye." Maxie hurried off knowing Jake was watching her. She tried her darndest not to trip.

* * * *

No sooner had Buddy closed the door behind the last committee member, than the sound he was dreading came.

"Buddeeeee!"

Oh, how he hated that sound. Sighing in resignation he turned around to face her. The look on her face said it all.

Both her lips and eyes were slits as she stood with her arms folded tightly over her ample bosom. As small as she was, to Buddy she looked like a steam roller about to flatten him. "I'm sorry, but didn't you see how he took control," he whined. Dee's expression didn't change.

"The guy has a hundred pounds on me!" he exclaimed, trying for pity.

Nothing from Dee.

To fill the silence, which he hated, he went on. "How was I to know he'd demand...

Dee started to tap one of her size four's, the toe making a tip, tipping sound on the thick square marble flooring in the hall. He waited until she stopped. Two could play that game.

"Yeah," he continued, "demand he do the mailing. You didn't see his crazy eyes!"

Dee would forgive him, but she'd make him suffer a little bit longer. "But you promised me, Buddy. You promised me."

She left him standing by the ornate double doors, looking small and wrung out.

* * * *

"Looks like you have an admirer," Mildred said as Maxie approached the car.

28

"Yeah, sure." Maxie shrugged it off trying not to show how flustered she really felt as she unlocked the car door. Pressing the button to unlock all the doors, she slid into the driver's seat. "All buckled in?" she asked, starting the car.

"How you doing Janet?" Maxie asked looking at her in her rear-view mirror. She thought Janet still looked a little flushed, making her beautiful gray hair even more outstanding. Maxie loved gray hair, but had to keep coloring hers as long as she could get away with it. When she was retired, then she'd let it go natural. Maybe.

"It was terrible." Janet put a hand to her throat.

"Did you see what I did to that table? It was actually pink."

Hearing the distress in her voice, Mildred turned partially around to look at her friend. "Janet, it was an accident."

"I know, but did I have to be drinking the red wine?"

Maxie couldn't help it. She started to laugh. Soon Millie was laughing.

"It's not funny! It's really not funny...".but Janet couldn't ignore the sounds of their laughter, and joined in.

Through fits of laughter, Maxie said outloud what they were all thinking. "If this is what we have to look forward to, I don't know... that room...that poor Buddy!"

* * * *

Mildred got into her own car that was parked in front of Maxie's house and waved as she drove away, filled with a sense of belonging.

She had forgotten how nice Maxie was, and wondered why they had lost touch. But then, wasn't that her biggest problem? she asked herself. Losing touch. This wasn't the same thing she told herself as she tried to put it out of her mind.

Mildred realized she didn't have too many friends. Some of her students still kept in touch, but that was with cards at Christmas.

Where had the time gone, she wondered. She knew that most of her time was devoted to her mother and she had no problem with that, but it was nice to be with old friends once again.

Enjoying the beautiful clouds in the sky added to her good mood, even if it had been spoiled by that dreadful man. She didn't want to think of that now and tried concentrating on Dee's Formal Room.

Now she had something to tell Ma, and she could hardly wait, it would give her mother a good laugh. Worry started to replace her good mood. Would she remember all of it, there was quite a bit, but then she remembered she did take notes.

And shame on Dee, treating Janet so unkindly. She shook her head at the thought. Poor Janet was just so upset when that wine went over.

She had to remember to tell Ma. Dear Ma, she'll probably get a good laugh out of that. She pictured Bella laughing.

She couldn't resist Ma's cackle. I wonder if I'm starting to sound like her when I laugh? Turning into her driveway, she was smiling to herself, anxious to tell Ma about the meeting.

Wonder how she did today? she asked herself. Bella had a phone right beside her on the table next to her chair. Her mother was getting so much weaker, so she made sure Angie their neighbor was home, if Ma needed help. She was a little apprehensive about leaving Bella alone, and never knew what she would find when she returned home. She rushed to the back door from the garage.

"Ma, Ma, I'm home," she called out, opening the door to the kitchen. Laying her purse and notebook on the table she glanced towards the front room.

She noticed Bella was not in her favorite chair in front of the TV. Maybe she's in her room, she thought. "Ma, where are you?" she called out again.

"Here Millerd," came Bella's reedy voice.

Mildred hurried to the darkened front room and looked around. "Where?" she asked again. Her eyes finally rested on the small form.

Bella was lying bunched up on her side, hard to see on the dark variegated beige carpet.

"Ma!" she cried, rushing to her. "Are you alright? Are you hurt? What happened?"

Bella didn't look up. Her gnarled fingers on her right hand held her head up off the floor, while her left hand feebly brushed at the carpet in front of her.

Mildred bent down and looked closely at her mother. "Can you move?" she asked worriedly, already feeling guilty for leaving her alone.

"Glad you home, I tired. Neck's tired, hold head up long time." She still did not take her eyes off the carpet. "Leg's give out, too weak. Hurry Millerd, get me up!"

"Why were you holding you're head off the floor like that?" she asked, helping her mother up.

"Didn't want them in my ears."

"What?" Mildred asked, puzzled.

"Ant's, Millerd, we got ants!"

* * * *

"Hi Martha, I'm home," Leon called out, looking around.

Now where is the old girl he wondered. "Martha, Martha!" he shouted even louder.

"I'm up here, quit shouting!"

"You wouldn't believe the afternoon I had," he said walking into the bedroom. Martha always seemed to be in the bedroom lately, with one complaint or another, so he failed to notice she was lying down with a damp towel across her forehead. "Boy, it was a doozy!" he exclaimed happily.

"Mmmm, could you keep it down please?"

"First of all," he went on enthusiastically, the house, you should see Buddy and Dee's house. Big, expensive house, and as that shit-head Gus said..."

"Please, Leon," Martha interrupted.

"Yeah right, sorry." Martha hated swearing.

"Anyway old Gus called it a fee, uh classy whore house. Thought I was gonna explode right there."

31

Sitting up on one elbow she pulled the cloth off her head. Squinting at her husband she asked, "What do you mean?"

"It's all white!" he shrieked.

"Leon!" she begged. "My head."

He finally looked at her. "Oh, you got a headache honey?"

Not bothering to answer him, she lay back and covered her eyes with the cloth.

"Anyway, everything, and I mean everything was white in that room. "The Formal Room," he said holding his nose and affecting a pose. "Even the pictures were white for God's sake. Did you ever hear of white pictures?"

Martha lay quietly.

"Poor thing, she didn't have a chance," he said running his plump fingers through his thick hair.

Pulling a corner of the cloth off her eyes and peering at him, she asked, "Who?"

"Janet, that's who. Poor kid."

Waiting for him to go on she studied him. Gone were the silk ties and button down shirts tucked nattily into pleated slacks. Since his weight gain he settled for loud printed silk shirts that encased his rather wide girth. Even his hair seemed to have shrunk on his fleshy-faced head.

She watched as he touched his shirt pocket reaching for the ever-handy cigar. "Oh no Leon, not now," she moaned.

"What?" He looked at her quizzically. His fingers unconsciously caressed the cellophane.

"The cigar," she pointed. She detested them.

His hand came back down, Martha breathed a sigh of relief. "What happened?" Martha asked raising herself on one elbow again, "You know, to Janet," she added squinting, trying to ignore the pounding in her head.

As if there had been no interruption he started, "She knocked over wine, and that piranha gave her a real bad time. She actually ran out of the room crying." He shook his head mournfully back and forth, then unexpectedly threw his head back and laughed, making Martha grab hers and hold on.

She wasn't about to ask what he was talking about.

"Leon, please," she begged, "my head."

He was still laughing when he continued, as if Martha hadn't said a word. "Well, I told you everything in the place is white, right?" He ignored Martha's long-suffering sigh.

"Well, when the wine went over, it stained this picky little table, and she was worried about that pukey green rug." He shook his head again. "You wouldn't believe it Martha."

She was completely lost. He could have been talking to a log. Martha decided not to move, hoping he would go away if she didn't ask anymore questions.

No such luck. He decided to plop down on the bed, jarring her head, her whole body and rattling her teeth.

She gave up. "Okay Leon, what wouldn't I believe?"

"The rug. It's lime, bright, bright lime, with ... I swear to you on my mother's grave," he said holding his right hand up, "it has orange and purple polka dots the size of balloons,"

Even though it hurt, it was Martha's turn to shake her head.

"And, if it wasn't for their tans," he paused, "they're heavy into all this trying to look young crap, you wouldn't be able to find them in that room."

Martha was floundering, but made an attempt. "The balloons?"

"No." He gave her a hurt look. "Weren't you listening?" "Buddy and Dee! They were all in white too!

* * * *

Gus sat watching, keeping his vigil from a safe distance in his beat up dusty brown van. It looked completely out of place in Buddy's high-class neighborhood.

He had been the first to leave, and now was able to study the others as they came out of the house.

He squinted in the bright low sun, facing it head on. He never wore sunglasses, never covered his eyes. Sunglasses were a government conspiracy, he believed, hiding the real things happening out there. He didn't trust the government, especially after he tried to save JFK.

"Eleven's, real eleven's," he said watching Mildred and Janet walk by. Seeing Maxie come out of the house and walk towards Jake who seemed to be walking towards her, he yelled, but not so anyone could hear. "Better watch out, she'll give you the clap!" He slapped his thigh at the joke.

He could handle the committee, especially Buddy. He makes it so easy he thought, but that 9525-ing Jake might just give him some trouble he imagined, his eyes taking in the scene.

But they'll see, all of them. He looked down at the folder in his lap and raised his fists in triumph. "I did it!" he said loudly. "I got the 9525-ing list!"

He smiled. "Those 9525-ing eleven's, they're not going to know what hit them."

* * * *

Janet did not bother to call out as she let herself into the quiet house. There was no one there waiting anxiously for her return, willing to listen to what she had to say.

Instead, she rushed to the bathroom, barely making it on time, unable to stop the drops that fell on the kitchen floor.

Janet sighed while wiping up the drips, her word for them. She looked around at where she had spent so many hours preparing wonderful meals with the fresh vegetables from her prolific garden. Now the kitchen looked cold and uninviting. Opening the refrigerator door half-heartedly, she leaned down pulling out the lasagna she prepared earlier and put it on the counter.

The wall clock read four-twenty-five. Godman liked to eat at five o'clock on the dot. Meals were dreary now, she felt. It was so much better when their son Christian was home. The last she heard from him, he was somewhere in the Congo doing God's work.

She repeated the prayer she made every day, "Please God, don't let anybody eat him."

34

Waiting for the oven to warm up, she went over the details of the day, cringing inwardly. She knew Dee had every right to be angry with her, but it still hurt that she was.

And Gus. *Look what he did today* she told herself. *He made fun of me and he doesn't even know me, for goodness sakes.* Not prone to feeling sorry for herself, she was surprised when her eyes started to sting, filling with tears.

What is it about me anyway, she wondered. *Andrew does the same thing, only he's not so honest about it.* The parishioners lap it up when he shrugs his shoulders as if he were a saint putting up with me. They actually smile, encouraging him.

Her dear father, she recalled, once called Andrew a pompous ass right to his face while we were all having dinner. Her father never came to their home again. The Godman forbade it.

She was tired of the hypocrisy, and she was lonely. The feeling Gus stirred in her were a little frightening, but not enough to keep her from looking forward to the next meeting, drips and all.

Heck, she said to herself, *I just need a little excitement in my life, just to get me through it. Is that too much to ask, Lord?*

BEFORE THE NEXT MEETING:

The small group from the committee checked out three different hotels, deciding on the Monarch. Outside of the lovely banquet room, the shuttle service from the airport helped them make their decision.

There would no doubt be out of town classmates and they wanted to make everything as convenient as possible. After all, they commented often, "It's our 50th, and nothing's too good for our 50th!" It became their slogan of sorts.

They had lunch in the hotel dining room to check out the food and met with a Ms. Keller, banquet co-ordinator. Selecting September 21, 1996 for their reunion, they agreed on a menu choice of Game Hens or N.Y. Sirloin.

Papers would be drawn up, Ms. Keller informed them, mailed of course to Buddy. They must be signed and mailed back with a $500.00 deposit within thirty days. They all agreed.

Ms. Keller reminded them that they had another thirty days after that to change their minds in order to receive a full refund. However, she cautioned, after that, the money would be forfeit. They understood and nodded solemnly.

Driving back to the park where their cars were parked, they felt a great sense of accomplishment.

"Lucky we still had a little over $700.00 left over from the last reunion," Dee said before getting out of the van.

"Nothing like seed money," she added, her dimples deepening as Buddy smiling at her, extended his hand to help her down. It had been a good day.

Jake and Mildred were waiting for them outside the van along with Leon who was unwrapping a cigar. Dee's dimples disappeared, replaced by a slight frown. Ghastly things, she thought.

"Jake, before I forget, could you and Mildred come up with an announcement that we could get out in the mail?" Buddy asked, still holding Dee's hand. "We have all the gear from the last reunions in a big box. We'll go through it at the next meeting and decide what we want to say."

Jake had enjoyed the day. This wasn't too bad, he thought. "Sure," he answered good- naturedly, the gentle breeze blowing his wispy gray hair in all directions.

"Yes, of course," answered Mildred. "And didn't everything go well today," she added. "So smoothly I thought. And I certainly enjoyed you're stories from you're salesman days, Leon. You were the life of the party."

"This is what it's all about," grinned Leon. "Getting together with good friends and having a laugh or two."

Smoke billowed around their heads from Leon's cigar. Pure contentment on his face proved too much for Dee.

"Leon!" Dee verbally pounced, "Do you have to smoke that awful thing now?" she shrieked, waving her arms around furiously to escape the nasty intruder.

Leon had been on a high all day, flushed with wonderful feelings towards these, his friends. They shared a common bond today, and he regaled them with his stories, just like he envisioned. He so loved being the center of attention.

Suddenly his cigar tasted flat.

"We can just move out of the way of the smoke, hon," Buddy suggested, pulling her away. Damn, he thought, seeing the stunned look on Leon's face. Just one day, one lousy day, that's all I ask.

THE MEETING: May 20th, 1995

Dee opened the door to Leon. The outside air was warm and sultry and Dee hurried him in. "Good, you're the last one, everyone else is here, come on in." To Leon, even that sounded like a rebuke from her, and he hesitated ever so slightly.

"Let's not let all this cool air out," she said, referring to the air conditioner humming away." She motioned for him to hurry, and hurry he did, for she was already closing the door.

Instead of going into the front room, which Dee had decided was now out of bounds to the group, especially Janet, he followed her down the hall to the family room.

He almost gasped at the colors leaping out at him as he entered. He didn't know if he should stand at attention or salute.

The overstuffed chairs were covered in alternating bold red, white and blue stripes or plaids. Little plump pillows shaped like stars, were placed everywhere possible.

When Dee finally decided on a motif for the room, which to no one's surprise was, The Patriotic Room, the lime green rug with the purple and orange dots, already covered the floor.

She had read somewhere that the carpeting in your home should flow, all one color and design throughout. She let it flow.

She also believed that when she had the red, white and blue plaid wallpaper added to the walls, with a border of large white stars on a dark blue background, no one would notice the carpeting.

The deliverymen who placed the new furniture in the room could hardly wait to make their escape.

Not so surprisingly, Buddy loved it too, for they had the same tastes. Whenever anyone asked, and they usually did, he lovingly referred to the fact that Dee was the sole decorator. All the furniture custom made to her specifications.

Dee had actually had the room photographed and mailed the glossies to House Beautiful, hoping they would do a spread on her masterful decorating.

The pictures, when received by the magazine, were tacked on a prominent bulletin board, with a message in bold letters: NEVER, EVER DO THIS!!! Then sent to their Museum of Bad Taste.

"Hi Leon," he heard as he plopped himself down on a bright red and blue striped chair.

"Yeah hi," he answered to whoever, reaching behind him to adjust one of those hard little pillows. Looking around, his jaw dropping a bit, he felt as if he were at a 4th of July parade and expected the fire engines to start blasting their horns.

"Jesus Christ," he muttered when he noticed the rug. That pukey green mixed with all these colors. He wasn't sure he could handle it.

"Did you say something Leon?" asked Buddy waiting for everyone to get settled. He thought Leon looked heavier.

Maxie, sitting the closest to Leon, heard him. She understood his dilemma. The room was closing in on her too.

"Oh, no. I just got a cramp in my leg, it happens sometime," Leon lied, rubbing his knee for show.

Maxie pinched herself hard, the laughter fighting to get out. God, she was going to be black and blue at this rate, she imagined.

Jake was sitting across from her on a huge sofa, a mischievous gleam in his eye. He was grinning at her, tapping one finger on the cushion as if to say, "Look at this!"

Dee outdid herself. It was no ordinary sofa. Covered in bright red corduroy, it had a large American flag design that fought hard with all the other stripes and plaids in the room. Lots of plump star pillows were tossed on just to make sure you got the message.

Maxie tried very hard to ignore him, but couldn't help grinning back. Everyone but the hosts she noticed seemed to be sitting stiffly, and turned like puppets towards Buddy as he started to speak.

"Okay, glad you could all make it," he began. "Everybody comfortable? Got something to drink?" He laughed. "I guess we don't have to worry about spilling anything in here, do we?"

His glance rested on Dee, and quickly moved on. She was not smiling.

He cleared his throat and took a quick look at Gus, who seemed unusually quiet. Maybe he died was his first thought. Fantasizing how it would solve a lot of his problems, the bubble burst. Dee would sure be pissed if it happened here.

A grip of paranoia engulfed Buddy as Gus moved and gave him a sneery grin. My God, he imagined, he knows what I'm thinking! He cleared his throat again.

His voice, when he spoke rang in his ears.

"On the 25th of last month, five of us went to the Monarch Hotel, one of three we checked out." He noted with relief, his voice was sounding more normal to him. "We decided it would be the best one since it was handy to the airport, and of course we liked the accommodations."

Settling down, he continued. "We picked September 21, 1996 for the date of reunion," he added with confidence.

"What about food?" asked Maxie.

Dee raised her hand as if she were in school. "We ate lunch there, the food wasn't too bad," she dimpled.

"What did you have?" asked Gus nonchalantly.

Everything seemed to stop. Dee exchanged glances with Buddy, then turned to Gus and asked, "What do you mean, what did we have?" a puzzled look on her face.

"What don't you understand about the fee-ucking question?"

The first to respond was Jake. Pushing himself off the couch and slowly straightening out, his face getting red, he moved towards Gus. His mouth was grim. "That kind of talk is not necessary Gus," he glared at the man.

Gus did not even bother to look up, he was still staring at Dee. Her eyebrows shot up into her hairline and her mouth was still open in disbelief. She turned to Buddy who seemed to be immobilized against the red, white and blue wallpaper.

"Buddeeeee!!!

"Jesus, okay...okay," he said slowly peeling himself away from the wall and hating his predicament. "Gus, this has got to stop... we don't need this crap!" was all he could come up with.

Mildred, sitting on the other end of the sofa from Jake, was jostled when he got up. She had been drifting, the voices lost in her reverie.

Confused and startled by the loud voices, she asked, "What happened? Why is everyone shouting?"

Leon was incredulous. "What do you mean, how could you miss what Gus said?"

"What, I ahhh" Mildred paled, realizing she had lost time. Concerned at Mildred's color and look of distress, Janet laid her glass down and crossed to Mildred's side. "Are you okay Millie?"

All eyes seemed to be on her, adding to her confusion. "Yes, yes of course, I'm alright," she said unsteadily but with as much dignity as she could muster.

Gus, forgotten for the moment, leaned back in the white chair with the wide blue stripes, his eyes dark and hooded. A smile played on his bluish lips. "Goddamn, I'm really sorry," he said slowly. "I just wanted to know what kind of food you all had. That's all. No need to get all those hot drops," he paused to let it sink in. "Now is there?"

He's doing it again, thought Buddy. The son of a bitch is doing it again. Heat seemed to rise from his chest to his brain, especially under his rug. He could barely control the impulse to snatch it off his head, or the uncontrollable rage that was building up. It was just too much.

Buddy's voice came out high, a pitch he never attained before, as he shrieked at Gus. "What are you nuts?" He had risen on his toes. "Who cares what we had for lunch?" On his toes Buddy reached the heights, five-foot, four and a half, a formidable opponent.

"We had fucking lunch, okay?" He was practically doing a pirouette.

Gus calmly raised his head and looked steadily at Buddy.

Dee could hardly believe her eyes. She had never seen Buddy act like that. She rushed up to him. "It's okay honey, calm down," she whispered. "It's okay." She began petting his back with small nervous strokes.

Trying to understand how things could go so wrong so fast, Maxie decided it was the room. It had to be. Coming at them from all directions, the loud colors clashing together, demanding attention. It has to be affecting all of us, she determined, we're jittery..but poor Buddy, he's a wreck.

What had she gotten herself into she wondered. Dee or no Dee, this just might be my last meeting. She thought of her grandson Jeezer, the real reason she was here. She couldn't abide that crazy loud music he and his band, "The Smokin Zebras," were playing. Always practicing in her garage on Saturdays... maybe I just need earplugs.

Maxie looked over at Jake. He had gone back to his seat, but was still glaring at Gus. She raised her eyebrows as he turned back to look at her. She smiled. He only nodded. Oh, oh, he's not a happy camper, she thought.

Sitting quietly through the whole exchange, Janet looked on, her only concern being for Mildred. She did not like to move too quickly now, and stayed next to Mildred on the couch.

Her incontinence caused her lots of discomfort, to both body and soul, but since she started wearing Depends, she felt more secure. However, she felt it was like having a water balloon between her legs, a little disconcerting, but certainly not unpleasant. She only worried that it might pop if it got full enough.

It made her think of the water balloon games at the church picnics, her favorite game. The erotic feel of the pliable balloon in her hands. Not something a Reverend's wife should notice certainly.

She remembered Andrew's stony stare as she held on to one a little too long, gently squeezing it over and over, then the water splashing into her shoes when she dropped it. She didn't miss Andrew's disgust, it was written all over his face.

Moving slightly, she adjusted her skirt, causing a pleasant feeling in her groin, making her giggle. She looked around quickly to see if anyone noticed. Only Mildred seemed to have heard and gave her a strange look, but then turned her attention back to the group.

Mildred was still in a daze. She felt foggy and wondered what had happened to her. It was unsettling to say the least. Everyplace she looked made her a little nauseous. All the stripes and plaids and dots jumbled together. She looked up and sighed, at least the ceiling is quiet.

"Well, ah, folks," said Buddy sheepishly, trying to get their attention. "I apologize for losing it like that." He gave them a sickly grin. "I don't usually get that emotional, honest, you can ask my wife," he looked at Dee. "Sorry everyone." He deliberately ignored Gus.

What a whiney 9525-er! Gus was enjoying himself.

"I don't know what you are apologizing about," Leon was indignant. "You have every right to get sore." He glanced at Gus as he nervously took a cigar out of his breast pocket and started to fumble with the cellophane.

His movement was not lost on Dee, who bolted out of her chair in a rush to confront him.

"What do you think you're going to do with that filthy thing?" she demanded, startling Leon in mid-rise of the cigar towards his gaping mouth.

"Don't think you're going to light that in my house!" she yelled.

"No, no of course not." He quickly began to stuff the cigar back into his pocket, unknowingly breaking off a large piece halfway down. "I just like to hold it in my mouth," he tried to explain. "It relaxes me. Sorry," he said embarrassed, not knowing where to put his hands.

When he had time to think about it later, he knew exactly where they should have gone. .

Buddy groaned. Oh hell, I just want this day to be over so I can go and lay down somewhere...and forget everything. He dwelled on that for a moment before asking, "What were you going to say Leon?" trying to get things back on track.

"I can't remember," Leon mumbled.

Gus cleared his throat, and even though nobody wanted to, they looked at him.

"Can we all just get on back to the fee-ucking meeting?" He smiled and slowly added, "I haven't got all day."

Past shock and well into resignation, an exhausted Buddy slowly bent down to pick up a folder he had forgotten he dropped earlier when everything hit the fan.

"Well, let's see." He began gathering up the papers from the folder. One crisis after another he thought. "Where were we?" he asked tiredly.

Dee stooped down to help him, unaware she was a big part of his problem. "Here you go honey," she whispered sweetly handing him a few sheets of paper. "Don't let him bug you."

Watching their every move through slitted eyes, Gus was thinking how goddamn pathetic they were. 9525ing elevens!

"Did you tell them about the food we had for lunch, Buddy?" asked Mildred thinking whatever just happened was over and she was contributing.

There was a stunned silence until Maxie, seeing the irony of it, looked at Jake and they burst out laughing. Leon's laugh was not too hearty, he was still seething from Dee's put down, but he joined in. Buddy and Dee, at first unable to see the humor, caught on and joined the others.

Janet smiled broadly. She loved to see people laugh.

Still feeling in the dark, Mildred decided to go along with the funny thing she must have said. "I'm sorry," she said, "Did we already cover that subject?"

The laughter became louder and much, much more relaxed.

Knowing he was the butt of the joke, Gus did not laugh at first. Then remembering he had the upper hand, he did have the list. So he let himself smile, a wide gargoyle smile.

Feeling the tension drain out him, Buddy began again.

"Nothing like a good laugh to ease the tension, is there? Thank you dear Millie."

She nodded, completely at a loss.

After that, things calmed down. They did manage to go over the wording for the announcement, checking the one used previously for their 45th reunion. Time, date and place were changed, plus who to send the checks to and where, along with the now dreaded menu.

Being the one in charge of having them printed up, Jake tried to be magnanimous. "How are the envelopes coming along Gus?"

"Well now, I've been working on them Jake, and as soon as you get those announcements ready, Jake, I'll get them all mailed out. Okay, Jake?" Each Jake was like a thrown dart.

Jake decided to ignore his down right nastiness. They'd all had enough for today. He knew he did. Buddy on the other hand had been holding his breath, waiting for Gus's reply, visibly relaxed.

Apparently he was numb, except for that Jake business, it wasn't too bad, he thought.

The only other problem arose after Gus's statement and Mildred's innocent question that followed.

"But don't you want help with stuffing the envelopes?" she asked, regaining her bearing somewhat. She looked in Gus's direction but didn't care to say his name.

Feeling threatened, Gus pushed himself halfway out of his chair. "Why? What's the fee-ucking problem?" he demanded, his large head thrust forward, dark eyes bulging. "Don't you think I can handle a simple thing like stuffing the goddamn envelopes?"

Mildred, terribly shaken, pushed her back against the sofa, as if to get away from him. She felt absolutely menaced by this horrible man.

Struggling to get out of the sofa and on his feet, Jake faced Gus again. "Wait just a damn minute. I think Mildred just wanted to help. Have you got a problem with that?"

Maxie was impressed, again, and Buddy was just glad he wasn't the one facing Gus.

Realizing he had overreacted, Gus decided to back off. This was not the time. He slid back in his seat, saying in a slow drawl, "Mildred, that is your name...right?"

Mildred could only nod, dumbfounded.

"Well, you see Mildred, I have a lot of time on my hands, and I hope you all will not mind if I do this one little thing. After all, they will be coming back to Dee, and this will be my only contribution."

He paused, turning his large head to one side, completely mesmerizing Janet, who wondered if the rest of his body was going to follow.

Gus looked at each one, taking his time. "Now that's not too much to ask, is it?"

They all stared at him. Mildred's skin crawled. Maxie was repulsed and Leon muttered, quietly, very quietly, "bastard!"

So far that was the longest sentence from Gus, and they waited, expecting the worst. That word.

But he fooled them and sat completely still. No one else moved or said a word, held captive by his strange behavior.

Look at these slobs, he told himself, keeping that creepy smile on his face. I got them eating out of the palm of my 9525-ing hand!

AFTER:

He had to get out of that house. Jake felt like he had been through the wars. He was not used to people hollering at each other or being nasty, especially in somebody's house. God, he missed Franny.

Barely saying his good-byes, he rushed down the dark hall towards the front door. He felt hot and clammy, even though the air-conditioner had been working most of the afternoon. It just wasn't the same as good clean fresh air and he had to have some.

This house, that God-awful room. How could anyone put those colors together and expect to feel comfortable, he asked himself as he stepped outdoors, sighing with relief.

Franny had always believed in simplicity. He loved what Fran had done with the rooms. Her mother's and grandmother's pieces fit in so beautifully. The few things from my family were welcomed and exhibited with pride. The pictures of relatives in beautiful old frames gave him comfort.

He couldn't remember if there were any pictures in that terrible room, but then he thought, who'd see them?

His thoughts switched to Gus. What is it with that man? He couldn't remember ever meeting anyone so deliberately belligerent, so awful.

There was something, however. He wished he could remember what exactly. It had been bugging him all day. Maybe, he told himself, if I don't concentrate on it, it will come to me.

He smiled, remembering how he and Franny were always forgetting a name of something or someone, and how they would try, but couldn't remember. And how, out of the blue a day or two later, one of them would recall and it would pop out of their mouths unexpectedly, making them laugh.

He breathed deeply of the outside air and took his time walking to his car. He hoped Maxie would follow, then almost immediately, he felt guilty.

As the ladies came out of the house, Mildred and Janet walking ahead of Maxie, passed Jake waiting by his car.

"See you next time Jake," Mildred said, thinking maybe she should thank him again, but decided against it.

Jake's eyes were on Maxie and didn't realize someone was talking to him.

"Jake?" said Mildred expecting an answer. "See you next time?" Like a typical schoolteacher, she waited for the answer.

"Oh yes, yes, see you next time." Then added to himself, maybe not. He turned back to watch Maxie fish around in her purse and come out with her dark glasses.

Seeing Jake up ahead and knowing he was watching her, flustered Maxie and she dropped her glasses. Bending down to retrieve them, she noticed he was walking towards her.

"Did they break?" he asked taking her elbow to steady her.

She dropped them again, feeling sixteen.

"Here, let me." He bent down slowly, picked them up and handed them to her.

Walking a few steps slightly bent over, he had some difficulty straightening up. She was tempted to put her hand in the middle of his back and give a gentle push.

"Thanks," she said taking the glasses from him. "I get butter fingered sometimes, but are you okay?"

"Oh sure." He smiled at her, which definitely did something to her heart. "Why?" he asked.

"I noticed you had a little trouble straightening up."

"Oh that. Would you believe that at one time I could leap over burning buildings in a single bound?"

They laughed.

"Maxie," he started, surprising himself as he asked her, "Would you like to have dinner with me tomorrow night?" Before she had a chance to answer he added, "I have to talk to somebody about this awful mess we're in. What do you say?"

She knew Jeezer had some kind of gig and she did promise to go. She was torn, but not for long. "Yes, I'd love to, that would be great." She shut her mouth before she went on and on.

"Is six too early to pick you up? I just can't eat too late anymore." His eyes looked so earnest. She liked that. "I'm awake all night if I do," he added.

"Perfect. I don't like to eat late either." She had small delicate ears, he noticed. "And on weekends I always try to have an early dinner," she said. He liked her mouth. "The rest of the week I can't manage it." He was looking at her steadily, making her a little nervous.

"What?" he asked. "What can't you manage?"

"With work and all," she explained. I can't eat early."

"Oh, that's right, you're still working." He hoped he didn't make that sound like she shouldn't be.

Maxie smiled at him. She decided not to go into it now.

She had written her number down, just in case. "Here's my phone number and address." She handed him a slip of paper she pulled out of her purse. "I really shouldn't keep Mildred and Janet waiting any longer." She touched his hand holding the piece of paper. "See you tomorrow night Jake. Bye."

"Bye," he said happily. He didn't feel the least bit guilty now.

* * * *

Still feeling the sting of Dee's wrath about his cigar, Leon could hardly be civil to her and muttered a quick good-by to them both and left.

He barely noticed Janet and Mildred and absently returned their wave. Opening the car door, he slid behind the wheel. As soon as he settled himself in he reached for the cigar in his pocket.

"What the hell!" he said, pulling out the stub. He patted down his shirt pocket feeling for the rest of it, wondering what had become of it. "God," he muttered, "the poor thing is probably laying on that pukey green rug." He smiled to himself. She'll probably have a shit fit when she finds that.

He lit the butt, puffing quietly, unaware of the cloud of bluish smoke surrounding him before it drifted out the open

51

window. Eyes narrowed in anger, he thought, who the hell did she think she was anyway? I wasn't going to light the damn thing, he told himself self-righteously. She could have waited to see what I'd do before she got her big tits in the wringer.

He pulled away from the curb slowly, forcing himself not to step on the gas.

Boy, has she got a mouth on her, he thought. Poor Buddy. It made him appreciate his Martha all the more. I know she hates my cigars too, but she'd never humiliate me like that.

He felt more than humiliated. She made a fool out of him, and made him look small in front of the rest of them. He could not forgive that. This was supposed to be fun, lots of laughs. "Ha! Some fun, some laughs! Getting yelled at like I'm some damn kid," he said to himself in the rearview mirror.

Anyone passing, and looking at Leon, would expect to see someone with him in the car. His head nodded and his free hand stabbed at the polluted air around him.

"And look at all the attention that shit head Gus gets!" he yelled feeling a pang of jealousy. At the thought of Gus he became so tense his shoulders were practically covering his ears. "Look what he did to Millie, for Christ sake!"

The smoke from his cigar was coming hot and heavy as he took deep angry puffs. "Everything the son of a bitch does, just beats the shit out of us. We're all a bunch of jerks letting him get away with that. What the hell does he want?" he asked the man in the mirror.

He didn't have an answer and clamped down hard on the butt bobbing in his mouth.

"I don't know if I can take anymore of these so called meetings." He slumped behind the wheel wincing again at the thought of Dee. "I can't take that broad, and I sure hate Gus's guts!" he shouted.

He really hated to admit it but he was intimidated by Gus who scared him, but then hell, so did Dee.

He stepped on the gas pedal as if to get away from his thoughts, but then he remembered how his friend had to deal with the two of them. He slowed down.

"Poor guy, poor bastard," he said quietly through the smoke.

* * * *

Dee glared at Buddy sitting slouched at the breakfast table. She felt all of it was his fault, he wasn't assertive enough. Why couldn't he be stronger, like Jake, she asked herself. Does he have to be such a wimp?

Of course she had felt bad for him today. She remembered how that awful, dreadful Gus gave Buddy such a hard time. She went up to him, didn't she? She stood by his side, didn't she? What more, she wondered, was she supposed to do?

She knew Gus intimidated him, and it bugged her. Why did she always have to yell at him to make him do the things she wanted. He should know already, my God we been together forever, I'm tired of looking like the bad guy all the time, she fumed, doesn't he see I'm sensitive?

He would have let that damn Leon light that damn cigar, I just know it, no one is supposed to smoke in that room or any other. And he knows it too. She glared at him sitting there feeling sorry for himself.

And that damn toupee that she had to keep checking for him. Christ she hated it and wanted to rip it off his head, but she knew the alternative would be worse. She glared again.

Buddy felt like shit. What is she giving me that look for, he wondered. Didn't she see what that guy did? Can't she tell I've got no control over him? He looked down at the floor wanting to shout at her, he's got us by the balls! He slumped lower in his chair. God, he thought, I don'know if I can take another meeting.

Going into the family room to pick up, Dee was starting to feel a little sorry for her husband. Walking across the floor, one of her size four's stepped on something. She jumped up and let out a shriek, thinking it was a mouse.

"What? What happened?" Buddy asked breathless from fear. He had rushed into the room to find Dee standing on the couch.

"What's that?" she demanded, pointing down at the short brown object lying among the polka dots.

He bent down to get a better look. "This?" He gingerly picked it up. "Why it's just part of a cigar." Relieved, he felt like laughing, until he looked up at Dee's face. "Leon must have dropped it."

"Leon!" she spat out. "Did you see him unwrap that awful cigar?" She had come down from the couch and was directing all her anger at "it", since Leon wasn't there. "The nerve, in our house yet!" she said incredulously. "He was going to smoke it too...who'd he think he was kidding?"

With her voice rising, Buddy's finger's holding the offensive object began to feel hot. He wasn't sure what he was supposed to do with it, however, an idea popped up as he glared back at Dee.

"But... he didn't light it, that's the main thing," Buddy tried to get across.

She'd have none of it. "But... he would have if I hadn't asked him not to, and you know it!" she said accusingly. "Right?"

He shrugged his shoulders, looking for a means of escape.

"Get rid of that thing!" she demanded, picking up a few glasses and heading for the kitchen.

He followed her and started to put it in the wastebasket. "Not there!" she ordered, as if he were a little boy.

"Where?" he was starting to get angry. "You want me to bury it in the back yard? Better yet, how about the dumps?"

"You needn't get sarcastic...now really."

She had the good sense to know she could only push Buddy so far and was smart enough to back off at a certain point.

Changing her tactics, she tried, "Honey," in a soft voice, walking across the room to stand close to him.

"What?" he asked sullenly.

"You know what...you forgot to tell them when the next meeting was going to be."

"I'm not sure there's going to be another one," he said quietly, not looking at her.

"Why, why would you say that? Of course there's going to be another meeting. What about the reunion?" She touched his arm, making sure he was looking at her. "What about all our plans?" she pouted.

He could hardly believe what he was hearing. Was she blind? "Didn't you see how bad it was today?" he asked.

"Well,... maybe. Just a few minor setbacks, that's all. But quickly reassuring him she added, "You were great, honey, standing up to him like that." She hugged him.

"I know that awful Gus was just awful, but you told him off, remember?" She dimpled sweetly at him. "He can't get the best of you, sweetie."

Oh, how he wanted to believe that. "Really hon?" he asked warily. He hated looking small in her eyes. "He did have me going there for awhile, you have to admit." He looked at her for confirmation and she obliged with a nod.

"But then you got it back on track, hon. Honest."

"Yeah, I guess I did." He straightened his shoulders a bit, feeling more optimistic about the past few hours, seeing it through her words.

"Of course you did sweetheart, you were wonderful." She was determined not to lose control, and if pumping him up was the way... well. "You know, and I know, anything worthwhile is never easy."

"You're right, I was pretty good today if I do say so myself." The weight that almost crushed him earlier was now miraculously lifted. The nightmare he lived through just awhile ago, diminished, leaving only an annoying residue. Maybe it really wasn't as bad as he thought. Hey, she was there, and she never lied to him. He could be easily led to her conclusions.

"Did you notice how everyone kept looking around?" she asked changing the subject, dismissing anything unpleasant. "They loved the room, I could tell. Couldn't you?"

"They looked alright," he agreed.

"We'll have the next meeting in there again. We don't want to disappoint them and besides...I love to see the envy on their faces." She was bursting with new plans and a great surprise.

"Yeah, you're right, the next meeting will be a lot better," he tried convincing himself. "A lot better I'm sure. Hell, it can't be any worse." He smiled at her, already seeing it in his mind's eye.

He loved being in control, it made him feel taller.

Dee smiled back. Satisfied.

* * * *

He was soaring, higher than a kite as he left the meeting. What a bunch of eleven's they all are, Gus thought. Buddy thinks he's running the show, but they found out differently, that's for 9525ing sure!

That Jake was a pain in the ass today, always butting his nose in. Thinks he's some kind of hero or something. That old guy can hardly straighten up. He laughed, trying to dismiss him.

But he remembered Jake at Spinning. Tall and strong, not easily intimidated. They had almost been friends once. He rubbed his head back and forth, putting the thought out of his mind with another one.

Nobody remembered him and that's what he was counting on, for as long as possible. He'd let them know when he was ready.

Heading home, he stopped first at a drive-through to pick up some chicken for his dinner, but he couldn't understand the young man with the broken English taking his order.

"9525!" he yelled into the microphone. "Nobody speaks any 9525ing English!"

He roared off, leaving a bewildered Pakistani asking, "9525?... Sorry?"

* * * *

"What happened to you today, Mildred?" asked Janet on the drive home from the meeting.

Mildred didn't turn around to look at Janet in the back seat. She had been thinking about the very same thing as she glanced out the window at the moving scenery. Unfamiliar places came and went.

"I really don't know," she said quietly. "It was weird. Suddenly there was all this commotion and I didn't know why," she said slowly, as if still trying to figure it out. "It was a short time apparently, but it was scary. I've had lots of moments of not remembering, but this was the first time everything just sort of disappeared."

"Have you been to a doctor?" Maxie asked, looking into the rearview mirror, catching Janet's eye. She saw the concern on Jan's face.

"My last physical was about nine months ago, and I did mention my forgetfulness."

Maxie looked over at her. "What did the doctor say about that?"

"That it wasn't anything unusual. The older we get, you know," she said without too much conviction.

"Yeah," they both said in unison.

* * * *

The first thing Maxie saw when she opened her front door was Jeezer sprawled on the couch. His wild mess of dark blond hair hung in swirls around his face. Bright blue bangs covered his eyes.

"Hi Grams! What's happening?"

"That's what I'd like to know," said Maxie, stunned at the sight of him. "When did you do that?"

"What?"

"Your hair," she pointed. "You look like some kind of... bird," finding the word she was searching for.

"Oh that," he shrugged his shoulders. "We were experimenting, and it just kinda got...fucked." He shrugged expansively again

She stared at him in disbelief. Of course he used that word, he's seventeen, she told herself, but never in front of her. She

57

couldn't see his eyes so she wasn't sure if he was surprised or not.

At least he pronounced it right, she had to admit. Not like that weirdo Gus. "I'll ignore that for now," she said, trying for authority, "but I don't want to hear that from you again young man."

"Sorry Grams," he said quickly.

He didn't sound too sorry, but now she just wanted to drop the whole thing and concentrate on something nice, like Jake, and Jake taking her to dinner tomorrow night.

"Well, I hope so, we'll just forget about it cause I've got some news for you. Believe it or not," she rushed on, "I've got a date!"

Seeing the word forming on his mouth, she screeched, "Don't you dare!"

"I was just going to say, for goodness sakes," he mocked. "Don't you think you're a little..." ?"

"Old!" she finished for him. "Get that hair out of you're eyes, I feel like I'm talking to a Shmoo."

"Well, aren't you?" he kidded, pushing the blue bangs to one side. "What's a Shmoo, anyway?"

"Never mind, but trust me..." she grinned at him. "You think older people don't date? It's just for dinner by the way, with a committee member."

"When's the date?"

She hesitated. "Tomorrow night."

"Geez, Grams!" he whined. "What about our gig at school, you promised."

"How about, I leave it up to you," said Maxie. "After all, I did promise you first." She waited, crossing her fingers behind her back.

He made her wait a good three seconds. "I think you should go on your old geezer date." Giving her a high five and a wide smile, he yelled, "That's rad, Grams!"

"What's that mean again?" she said raising her hand and slapping his in the salute.

"Good, Grams. That means real good!"

She really loved the little stinker, blue hair and all.

* * * *

Jake glanced at his watch. It was six o'clock straight up, as he parked in front of Maxie's house. He liked being punctual and got slightly annoyed when others weren't.

Nice little home, he thought. It looks inviting. He noticed Petunias and Impatience blooming in the flower box under the large picture window.

Two mature Camphor trees on either side of the front walk shaded the home perfectly from the late afternoon sun.

To his surprise and delight, the front door was opened by Maxie before he had a chance to ring the bell.

She was smiling as she held the door open. "Welcome, Jake." She had a chance to look him over as he walked up to the door, and up close he looked even better. His brown and white small checked jacket and tan slacks looked sharp with the light beige shirt and brown tie, even though he looked a little stiff.

Assuming it had been a long time since he put on a tie, she was flattered.

Jake had been looking her over too, and was so pleased to see she was wearing a dress, instead of the customary slacks most women opted for today.

The color intrigued him, a soft gray green, which certainly complimented her curly hair and dark brown eyes. He had a hard time tearing his eyes away from the rest of her.

"Hi Maxie," he smiled back. "You look lovely." Stepping inside, he glanced around approvingly. "You have a lovely home here." He took in the neatness of the comfortable front room.

Maxie tried to see it through his eyes, looking at the pale beige walls and carpet, the muted brown paisley sofa and woven cane chairs, with live plants in baskets.

"Thanks, at least it's mostly all one color. Bland."

He laughed softly, "And it's most gratefully appreciated."

"Could I get you something to drink, wine or something non-alcoholic?" she asked. She noticed he was still standing and decided he was probably anxious to get going.

"If you don't mind, I think I'll wait and have some wine with dinner. I don't drink that much, but I do like a nice wine with my meal."

"Sounds great. Shall we go then?" she asked, picking up her purse from the wall table.

"Fine, I have reservations for six-thirty at Luigi's. I hope you like Chinese?" he said as he followed her out the front door, heading for his parked car.

She shot him a look of mock surprise as he held the door open for her. "I'm Italian, what else would I like?"

They were laughing as they put their seat belts on for the ten minute ride to the restaurant.

This was already fun she thought, and found him easy to talk to. They kept up the repartee' in the car, the kidding gentle and enjoyable.

She wondered as she sat across from him over the candlelight table, why she had been so nervous about this evening.

Jake was enjoying himself too, more than he ever thought possible. He had been nervous too, and still was a little, but it was the nice nervous, the energy kind. He felt his sense of humor returning in a rush.

He liked that she laughed easily and had forgotten how much fun it was to tease and be teased, to flirt.

"Well," said Maxie looking around at the checkered tablecloths and the candles dripping down the wine bottles. She picked up the large Italian menu, opened it up and scanned the entrees. "Let's see, I wonder how their Egg Foo Young is here?"

"Okay, okay, you win!" said Jake laughing. "Let's get that next time." It warmed him, just the possibility of a next time, something to look forward to. "I feel like a little parmigiana, how about you?"

"Sounds good. Gosh," she said checking the menu. "Salad, pasta, soup," she looked at him wide eyed. "I'd forgotten how much food they give you here."

"We'll just taste a little bit of everything," he said, rubbing his hands together as if he could hardly wait to get started. His eyes were sparkling as the waiter approached their table.

Through the pasta they exchanged bits of their history, where reluctantly she told him of asking her husband of ten years to leave. Of raising her four children alone, with no help, financially or otherwise from him. She did not tell him of Boris, her first love, or that she compared him to every man she ever met.

She talked of her job, skimming over the whys and wherefores, and how hard it was at times. "The young people of today seem brilliant," she said. "Maybe it's just that it's so hard sometimes to keep up with them," she added, her shoulders sagging a little.

"You must be very good at your job," Jake said. "There is so much going on out there, and it changes so quickly, too. My sons have made many changes in the shop." He shook his head. "They had to just to stay alive."

She nodded in understanding. "I just want to work a year or two, and then," she smiled broadly. "I'm going on a cruise!"

Through the soup, they talked of their children. By the time the salad arrived, they were warmed by the company, the wine and their surroundings.

The candle flickered on the table, casting long shadows on their upturned faces. The room became intimate and soft voices drifted in and out of their silences.

Jake shook his head in wonderment. "How did you ever manage all that?" he asked seriously.

She looked up from her salad, a smile playing on her lips. "What, all that food? So far it's been delicious."

"No, I mean raising four children by yourself. It had to have been difficult." His eyes locked onto hers. "My gosh, we only had two boys. I can't imagine what hardships Franny would have had to go through if she had been left alone." His eyes seemed to go inward as if he were imagining the possibility.

Maxie had had this conversation quite a few times before, and mostly hated to talk about it. But she didn't mind his comments. Hardships, he had said. Yes, yes, she remembered.

"You just do it, and fortunately for me, they're wonderful kids."

"Maxie," he said softly. "You're an amazing woman, you know," then looked down, embarrassed.

Noticing his discomfort, she tried to change the subject. "Look at this salad, they sure give you enough." She dug her fork into a crisp piece of lettuce.

"You know Jake, I'm really thinking about getting out of that committee. It's getting ridiculous. Gus is just too much. There's something definitely wrong with that man."

Jake had looked up when she started to talk. His eyes opened wide in surprise.

"I was thinking the very same thing yesterday." Shifting in his chair, he put his elbows on the table. "You know, I just had to get out of that house. I don't think any of us need those problems at this particular time in our lives. We need..." he paused, "serenity." He smiled. "Boy, that's an old man's wish, isn't it?"

"No, I think it's any sane person's wish." She leaned forward in her chair. "I know I've got better things to do with my couple of days off." She shrugged her shoulders.

Jake nodded. "You know, I was really invited to join because I'm a, or had a printing shop. I know Buddy, but we were never that thick in school." He moved a fork closer to his dish. "Now Leon, that's different."

"How? Maxie asked.

"Buddy and Leon were in the Hi-Y together. They've been good friends," he hesitated. "Of course I don't know if they see each other socially or not." He laughed at something.

"What?" she asked grinning.

"I'm sure you noticed there's no love lost between Dee and Leon," he said.

She began to laugh. "I actually felt sorry for him and his cigar, he got so flustered."

Jake was chuckling. "Can you blame him? She's really something, isn't she?"

"You know what?" she said devilishly. "We were best friends in school."

Jake quickly sobered. "Are you kidding? Oh, I'm sorry." Then he noticed the twinkle in her eyes and realized she was kidding him. "You're not real best friends now...are you?"

"No. I hope I've matured a little bit more."

"Believe me, you have, and very nicely."

She liked that, then turned serious. "What about Gus?"

"I'm not sure how he even heard of this. Maybe Buddy called him too!"

"Do you honestly think so?" She laid her fork across her salad plate. "I can't imagine them ever being friends, he really is terrible to Buddy." She frowned slightly. "I can't remember him in school. Are we sure he went to Spinning?"

"You know, it's funny, but I've been trying to remember something. It's close but I just can't get a handle on it." His face looked puzzled. "Gus looks like no one I remember, but there is something about him that's familiar."

"Really?" Maxie was fascinated. "I don't ever remember seeing him at any of the other reunions, and I've been to all of them. No, wait," she tapped her head. "Not all, I did miss the tenth one, I think."

"Fran and I went to all of them, She was two years behind us."

"Really, what was her name?"

"Frances Jean Spangler."

Maxie noticed how softly he said her name. "I'm sorry, I don't think I knew her. I wish I had."

"She was so pretty and so sweet. We were perfect together." He said it so wistfully, Maxie felt a stab of jealousy. She wished she had been loved like that. She dropped her eyes, seeing the moisture that gathered in his.

"Sorry," he said gruffly. "I still miss her so much."

"You know what Jake?" Maxie smiled at him. "You're pretty amazing yourself." She touched his hand, letting it linger.

Jake tried to grin, the tears in his eyes glittering. "I think," he said trying to get back to their former mood. "We'd better start on our salads. They're gonna wilt." He picked up his fork and dug in.

"Have we decided what we're going to do about the committee? You know for old Spinning High, The Top?" Jake asked between chews.

"Buddy and Dee certainly need help." Maxie tried to sound non-committal. "And didn't Gus say he was just going to do the mailing and then he would be through with his part?"

"Yes, I think you're right. I was so mad I could barely concentrate on the goings on." He touched her hand, thinking he could get used to this. "Yes, I think he said that," he said sounding hopeful.

She didn't move her hand. "Well, if we can put up with it through the mailings, Good Lord willing and the creek don't rise, it should be a piece of cake after that." Even after all those cliché's, she had a satisfied grin on her face.

"Good Lord willing," he repeated. "That's the key."

"The salad was delicious." She wiped the corners of her mouth, surprised at her appetite. "Bring on the parmigiana, it looks like we're not done yet!" She grinned at Jake then grinned wider at the look he gave back to her.

* * * *

After the last meeting with the committee, Mildred was more than a little concerned about the blackout or episode as she called it, but there had been no others in the last month, she hoped is was just a one time thing.

Mildred was dreading Bella's doctor appointment later that morning. Ma was getting harder to handle and her legs were so weak she could barely stand on them. Mildred had to lift her in and out of the car.

"The Tank," as she referred to her old Lincoln Town car, was waiting in the driveway. Mildred did remember to pull the car out of the garage this time. It was too big for the small one car garage, but she couldn't bear to part with it, it gave her such a feeling of security to drive it.

Since there was so little room to open the doors on either side, it was a struggle to get Bella in the car.

Helping Bella get dressed, she said, "Ma, I think today you should just wear your robe over your underwear. It's really nice outside and I think you'll be more comfortable. Besides, it won't be so much trouble to undress for the doctor."

"You sure, Millerd?"

"No one will even notice, it will be fine." But what Mildred did notice was how big the boxy robe had become on Ma. She must remember to buy her a smaller size, she told herself.

The doctor as usual, wasn't too encouraging and didn't give her any new news. Bella, she was told, would get weaker until she was permanently bedridden. Something Mildred had heard before but couldn't bear to think about it.

Turning into their driveway, Mildred pushed the button on the garage door opener.

"Millerd," Ma said.

"What Ma?" She looked down at Bella who seemed to have shrunk on the way home.

"I gotta pee."

"Okay Ma, I'll get you out of the car, hold on." Forgetting about the tight squeeze and thinking only of Ma's problem, she inched the car carefully into the narrow garage.

Mildred squeezed out on her side and sidled around the car to the other side.

Intent on her quest she barely noticed how close she was to the wall as she tried with difficulty to open the door on Bella's side. She was just about to suggest she drive the car out again, when Ma said, "Hurry Millerd," Bella said all scrunched."I gotta go... real bad."

Mildred's good idea went right out of her head. Instead, she made a grab for Bella, pulling her up off the front seat, believing she had a good hold under her mother's arms.

With so little room the heavy door compressed Mildred's shoulders and head. She felt a pressing pain in her neck.

Straining, she got Bella in an upright position out of the car. Bella, her arms over her head, her back to Mildred, slid like quicksilver out of her grasp, continued downward and disappeared.

With her arms extended out in front of her inside the car, Mildred realized she was holding an empty robe. Standing in a cramped position, wedged as she was against the car door and wall, she was unable to bend down to see where Bella was.

"Ma, where are you?" Mildred asked mystified, checking the floor inside the car, the only place she could easily see.

"Here," came a muffled voice.

"Where?"

"Under car!"

"But how?"

"Dunno!"

Stunned, but soon seeing the absurdity of the moment, Mildred burst into laughter. Soon, Ma was cackling along with her, the sound like something tinny down a well.

Feeding upon each other, the laughter continued. Mildred could no longer control her bladder and strong spurts ran down her legs and into her shoes. "My God, I'm peeing!" she gasped between spasms of laughter.

Weak from laughter, Mildred started to ease her way around the car. Walking stifflegged, so as not to feel the wet cloth of her slacks against her legs, she called out, "You okay Ma?"

There was no sound as she managed to get down on her knees and peer under the car. Ma, no longer laughing, was lying on her back, her head turned in Mildred's direction. She was staring at her with dark beady eyes.

To Mildred, it looked huge under that car and Ma looked so tiny. Of course, thought Mildred, she's right smack in the middle where I can't possibly reach her. Now how did she do that, she wondered.

"Millerd, Millerd" Bella shouted, sounding agitated. "Get me out!"

"Okay, I will," said Mildred assessing the situation. "Hold on."

"Bully Sheet!" Bella answered.

"Okay, Ma, okay." This was not going to be easy, Mildred realized, becoming aware of her knees. They were killing her pressed against the cold cement, pains shooting in all directions. She wondered if she would be able to get up.

She was still holding Bella's robe in her hand. Ma must be cold lying on the cement, she thought. "Here Ma, grab hold of you're robe and try to cover yourself," she said making a ball of the robe and tossing it under the car in the general direction.

It hit Bella's hand and she pulled it back as if she'd been stung. "It's wet!" she complained.

"Everything's wet Ma."

She had to think but her thoughts became sluggish as she tried to concentrate. It never crossed her mind that she should go get help. Instead, she mulled over ideas.

Maybe, if Ma lies real still, I wonder, she mused. I could drive straight out with out running over her. "No!" she said loudly. "Bad idea! The fumes would probably do her in!"

"What?" said Ma.

Suddenly, there was nothing. Time stopped for her. Seconds later into her consciousness she heard, "Millerd, Millerd! What are you doing?"

Mildred shook her head, the pain in her knees excruciating. She collapsed onto her side taking the pressure off. When she managed to stretch her legs out, she began rubbing her knees vigorously, the pain bringing her back to the moment.

Trying to concentrate, she looked around at her surroundings trying to remember. Finally recalling her mother's words, slowly said, "Hold on Ma, I'm working on it."

Exasperated, Bella said as loudly as she could. "Bully Sheet!"

"Will you quit saying that. It doesn't help anyone!"

"Me.... It help me." Bella said sullenly. "Just do something, Millerd."

Grabbing hold of the door handle, Mildred pulled herself up. Luckily, she thought, there was a handle, not something recessed into the door like the newer cars. She hobbled round, not noticing the heavy wet slacks until she got some feeling back into her legs.

"Alright," she called out. "Ma, can you roll over towards me? To you're..." she had to check her hands to see which was which. "Left?"

A moment later Mildred heard a thud, followed by, "Sheet!" as Bella apparently hit her head or something on the undercarriage of the car.

"What happened?" Mildred bent down again to look under.

"No room."

"Well, try using your arms to push towards me. I know you don't have much strength, but try. Please, Ma."

It physically hurt her to tell her mother to try it, but she didn't know what else to do.

Mildred got back down on the floor, lay on her side and looked under the car. Reaching out to her mother, she realized her arm wasn't long enough.

Powerless, she watched as Ma inched a little closer, shoving with her weakened arms and hands. What a trouper, she marveled.

After what seemed an eternity, she could get hold of Bella's left hand. Pulling slowly, Mildred managed to get her mother close enough for her to grab some of Bella's underwear. Slowly, slowly she pulled her out. Both were panting as they lay on the floor. Mildred cradled her mother's head in her wet lap, resting from the exertion.

"My robe, Millerd," Bella managed, feebly trying to cover herself.

Mildred barely had the energy to look under the car. The robe was there, bunched up near the middle. "Not now, Ma. I can't get it out now. Let's just try to get into the house."

"But they see me."

Mildred just wanted this over. "No one will see you, I promise," she said patiently looking down at her mother.

Bella looked pathetic. Her knit camisole covered her small sagging breasts, and the long nylon drawers with the wide legs, lay in folds against her thin wrinkled thighs. Brown nylon knee-highs sagged and twisted on her pencil thin legs. Luckily Bella still had on her maroon felt slippers, Mildred noticed. Praise the Lord I don't have to retrieve them from under there, she thought.

Bella, covered with oil stains, looked down at herself. "I dunno, I don't like it. I almost naked." She looked pleadingly at Mildred. "Someone for sure see me. But, I sure got to pee!"

Surprised that Ma had been able to hold it through all of this, she looked down at what her lack of control did to her tan slacks. "That's the only problem I don't have at the moment."

The thought of getting the wheel chair out of the trunk was exhausting. Between the two, she reckoned Ma was probably the lightest for her to handle.

As Mildred half carried, half-dragged Bella out of the garage into the bright daylight, a creaky voice shouted, "How-do, Ladies," as they headed towards their back door.

It was their eighty-year-old neighbor, Mr. Mahoo, leaning heavily on his cane, in their driveway. His arthritic shoulders stooped, his shoes full of intentional holes to let his bunions breathe, he nonetheless had a wide toothless grin on his wizened face.

Although he was partially deaf, his eyesight was still pretty good. Unfortunately for Bella, his blue eyes glittered at the sight he beheld.

Never one to ignore a friendly overture, Mildred turned to face him, turning Bella with her. "Afternoon, Mr. Mahoo," she answered, returning his smile.

Bella, helpless, could only stand there. But under her breath she managed a quiet, "Bully Sheeeet!"

* * * *

"You've got the Ladies Auxiliary on the 15th," said Andrew, walking into the room where Janet was sitting on the couch. "The choir's potluck, and Janet, are you listening to me?" he demanded. He noticed she was not looking at him as he expected. Instead, her back was turned towards him as she gazed out the window.

Her thoughts were elsewhere. On Gus. The last meeting. As time went on, she convinced herself he really didn't mean to be so mean. He was probably just a lonely man, she told herself. The church had taught her to reach out to those in need and she felt she could not turn her back on him.

"Did you hear what I just said?" asked Andrew. "You seem to be out in left field a lot." An expression he favored, even though he was not a baseball fan.

His voice was pulling her away from her thoughts, and unwillingly she answered him. "Yes, I heard you Andrew. Ladies Auxiliary, choir potluck and whatever," she repeated without enthusiasm.

The creases between his eyes deepened, as he became angrier. "What's wrong with you? Don't you understand you're here to help me do God's work?" He stared at her back. "And lately," he paused for effect, "you haven't been doing a very good job."

Janet continued to stare out the window. "Sorry," she answered barely audible.

"Sorry? Did you say sorry? Sorry is not acceptable, Janet," he said nastily, walking towards her.

He glanced at his watch. "My golf game starts in two hours and I still have my sermon to write." Impatiently, he began tapping the pen he was holding against his open palm. "I shouldn't have to spend this much of my valuable time with you." He moved closer until he was standing over her. "You know my work is most important. Why do you do this to me?"

Turning her head slowly, she looked up at him. "Do what to you, Andrew?" She stared back at him.

Becoming somewhat flustered at such insubordination from her, of all people, he stuttered, "Thi, this!" Waving his arms about the room, he added, "make me go on and on. I simply want you to take care of the Ladies Auxiliary and the choir. Do you think you can handle that?" he asked sarcastically.

She turned her back on him again and looked out the window. "Have you ever taken care of the Ladies of the Auxiliary, Andy?" she asked, turning to look up at him. Without waiting for an answer, she added, "I'm sure you have."

Andrew's face reddened. "How dare you!" he sputtered, feeling dread for the first time at Janet's assertiveness.

"I dare!" she said standing to face him. "I dare!" she repeated, as she turned and left him.

He stood staring at her straight back disappearing through the doorway, and for the first time he was speechless.

MEETING: August 12th, 1995

The day was hot. The temperature was expected to go into the low 100's, but Buddy and Dee were ready. The air conditioner hummed out cool air and there were plenty of cool drinks for the committee.

Lurking by the front door, Dee waited for the girls. "Where are they?" she said looking at her watch. She was dressed in shorts and halter-top, backless high heels on her dainty feet, while large silver hoops hung from her ears. At least a dozen bangle bracelet ran up one arm and rings adorned each finger.

Ready to burst with her surprise, she wanted them there now. The guys were already back in the family room, and of course she took note of their comments.

"Jeez, Louise!" from Leon.

She giggled remembering how Jake had asked her, "Shall we dance?" It was so cute she favored him with one of her deepest dimpled smiles.

"What the FEE-UCK? From you know who. She decided to ignore the remark, determined not to let him or anybody else upset her in the least. This is going to be a perfect day she told herself.

Maxie had picked up Mildred and Janet as usual. In the first silence since they got into the car, Maxie asked, "You know what?"

"What?" they both answered.

"I hope it's not going to be in that room again. That Patriotic Room." Millie and Janet laughed. "God, it's over-crowded, over-stuffed, way over plaids and stripes"...Maxie took a big breath, "and really overbearing."

"How did you think of all those words?" laughed Janet.

"It was easy," Maxie said. She rubbed her temple with her free hand, feeling a slight headache starting from Mildred's rose scented perfume. Mildred must have forgotten again. Maxie had told them both that she was highly sensitive to fragrances. Now, making her more uncomfortable, the hot leather seat

73

caused her blouse to stick to her back. Always a problem in hot weather.

"I'm so glad you said something," Mildred said. She didn't want to gossip since they were all friends, but now she added, "I honestly think it was that room that made me have that... episode." She was still avoiding the word blackout.

"You just have to face it guys, Dee has terrible taste," agreed Janet. "We just have to face it," she repeated. She leaned forward pulling her blouse from her wet sticky back. "Boy, it's really hot. Doesn't you're air conditioner work, Max?"

Feeling Janet's hot breath on the back of her neck, Maxie moved slightly forward. "Oh, I'm sorry. Of course you want the air on." She pushed and flipped buttons, adjusting the vents away from her. She loathed air conditioning, especially in the car, where she couldn't get away from it.

"It's blowing right on me," complained Mildred. "Could we adjust it somehow?" she asked putting her hands to her hair. Short gray tendrils were blowing in all directions. "It's messing my hair, and I just had it done!" she shrieked.

Maxie fiddled with the button, trying to keep her eyes on the road. She put the vents straight in the middle and Janet's, "Oh, that's better," told her at least someone was happy. She would just have to put up with it for a few more miles, even though it was raising hell with her head.

The short distance from the car to the house was wilting. The midday sun could easily have fried an egg on the sidewalk, and quickly dried the wet stains on their backs.

The door flew open before they could reach for the bell, saving them from an "Oh What A Beautiful Morning" refrain. Dee was all-aflutter, hugging each one as they entered into the welcoming coolness of the dark foyer.

"Hurry, hurry, I've got a great surprise for you!" she gushed. While Dee prodded them on, they stumbled and tripped trying to adjust their eyes from the bright outdoors.

Maxie could see a strange glow up ahead and stopped dead in her tracks at the family room entrance, causing the others to run into her and each other.

"My God," a stunned Maxie said, putting her hand to her temple and pressing. "What is this?"

Little squares of golden light rolled over everything and everyone like a merry-go-round gone amok. The only thing missing was the music.

Dee couldn't stand it, she had to ask. "Don't you just love it, the mirrored ball and the lights?" Her bangled bracelets clanged together as she clapped her hands in delight. Practically jumping up and down on her little size fours, she informed them, "I found it at garage sale, and I just knew we should try it out today and use it again at the class reunion."

It made Maxie sick to her stomach. Forms on overstuffed furniture seemed to be locked in time. Without saying a word, Mildred and Janet moved gingerly, feeling their way to a seat, while Maxie stood unsteadily, the sensation of standing on sand with receding waves undermining her footing.

Forget friendship, forget good manners, this was self-preservation, Maxie told herself. The heat, Mildred's perfume, the damn air conditioner, and now this. It was a conspiracy, giving her one gigantic headache. She grabbed Dee's arm to steady herself. "I can't handle this Dee!"

There was a heavy pause.

"What do you mean?" asked Dee.

"This, the lights...it's too much," complained Maxie.

"You don't mean you don't like it?" Dee asked in a wary voice.

"It's awful," stressed Maxie.

"Are you sure?" whined Dee.

A strong "YES!" came from different parts of the semi-darkened room.

"Well!" Dee said indignantly. "Some friends you are, I was trying to make this fun for all of you," she said sounding hurt.

"Dee, it's just"...Janet said trying to ease the situation.

"Never mind," Dee interrupted, already walking towards Buddy, hunched down in one of the chairs, trying his best to become invisible.

"Buddy, where's the damn switch?"

75

"Oh shit!" he muttered to himself, leaping up out of the chair. He did try to tell her that maybe it was too much when she came up with this idea. But no, she had to have it, and now I'm never gonna hear the damn end of it.

Quickly switching to his everything is okay mode, and even humming a few bars of a popular song, he turned off the spotlights and stopped the spinning ball. Then opened the drapes.

A collective sigh and one snore was heard as sunlight poured into the garish room, making everyone squint.

"For Christ's sake!" said Leon in disgust, looking at Gus.

Sprawled in a corner chair with his head back, eyes closed and mouth open, Gus appeared to be sleeping. Actually, he succumbed to the spinning lights and had fallen into a deep hypnotic trance.

"Maybe he died," whispered Mildred, getting up and walking slowly and with great trepidation towards him.

Another snore erupted.

"No such luck," said Leon sarcastically.

Gus was not a pretty sight and even Janet was a little repulsed. They all moved closer, watching him. His snores, though getting louder, were farther apart and he seemed to stop breathing between them. Some held their own breaths, getting panicky, waiting for the next one.

"Ni...fi..."

"He said something," Jake said, leaning towards Gus, "listen!"

"Even in his goddamn sleep he hogs all the attention," muttered a disgruntled Leon.

They leaned closer. All except Dee. She was pouting and was fed up with all of them and wanted them out of her house.

A loud snore startled the committee members and they backed away quickly, but after a few disquieting seconds they leaned back in again to hear a mumbled, "Enti...fi..went...fiii…"

It was barely audible and some dismissed it as nothing at all.

Mildred was intrigued. "What was that?" she asked. "Sounded like ine, if, or something."

Maxie was losing interest. "I don't think so," she said turning away. Her head was still pounding and she was ready to go home.

"Wait, wait," Buddy said quietly. "I heard it too, he said something that sounded like a number, maybe."

Another loud snore ripped through the room.

"Buddeeee, do something!" said Dee through clenched teeth.

"Shhh!" he replied.

That did not go over too well with Dee. She despised being shushed and demanded, "I want this to stop...now!

"Honey, wait a minute, please," he begged.

"Einty...if...oo...fif, ni..fi..to.." came from Gus's blubbery lips.

Buddy motioned them to get back. "Come on, let's leave him alone." Suddenly he realized this was a golden opportunity. "Maybe we could go outside," he whispered hopefully.

"It's too hot!" snapped Dee. Everything had gone to hell, her wonderful surprise that nobody appreciated. It was all Maxie's fault and she hated her at this moment, her eyes shooting daggers in Maxie's direction. She could no longer maintain any semblance of perkiness or enthusiasm she knew they expected of her. After all, she told herself, I just can't be sweet all the time.

Buddy was checking his watch. "We've already lost fifteen or twenty minutes. We could be having this meeting around the pool." His eyes implored Dee. "It could be nice and cool there honey."

Without waiting for Dee's permission, the committee filed out to the pool area, happily leaving the snoring Gus behind.

It wasn't very cool, but it was shady and even the hot breeze was an improvement over that room and Gus.

Slipping off her sandals, Maxie rolled up her pant legs and sat down at the edge of the pool. Dangling her feet in the cool water, she cooed, "Mmmm, nice."

Jake had not said a word to her since she walked through the door even though they had had several dinners together since the last meeting. Walking over to her, he slipped off his loafers and socks and joined her at the pool's edge.

With some difficulty he managed to sit down, feeling old and a bit creaky as he began to roll up his pant legs.

"Hi," he said, a satisfied grin on his face as he put his feet into the pool. "Here we go again. Do you believe what just happened in there?"

She had to laugh. Just seeing him made her feel better. At least for the moment, her head had stopped throbbing. We're simpatico, she thought enjoying the attention.

She leaned close to him and whispered, "I couldn't stand it in there. I thought I might faint."

"To tell you the truth, I thought I had come to a prom," he whispered back. Maxie giggled.

"I know she's you're friend, but what's wrong with her?" Maxie had to laugh but couldn't answer. Others were following her lead and came to sit on either side of them.

Leon sat down on a chaise and removed his shiny brown wing tips. He rolled his perfectly creased slacks to his knees, exposing short skinny legs. Jake and Maxie exchanged glances as he removed his shear knee-hi socks and carefully rolled them into a ball, stuffing them deep into the toes of his shoes, and placing them out of harm's way under the chaise.

Maxie had to look away as he walked to the pool's edge. His feet were tiny and delicate, all pink and puffy. She wanted to laugh, because of his round body, stick legs and fat feet, he looked like Mickey Mouse.

Suddenly she felt her arm being pinched and jumped.

"OW!" she said, rubbing her arm and glaring at Jake in surprise.

"Sorry, but you were about to laugh...weren't you?"

"Right, but," she didn't finish, just continued to rub her arm. Not because it hurt that much but at the anger that arose in her. She did not like to be pinched. Whatever possessed him, she wondered. This kind of attention she didn't need.

"Maxie?"

Not trusting her voice, she took her time turning to look at him.

"I shouldn't have done that Maxie. It wasn't my place and I'm really sorry. I just got carried away in the moment... I knew if you laughed, I would too. I'm really sorry."

His expression was so pitiful she had to relent. But when she touched his arm, he jerked it away. She laughed. "Did you think I was going to pinch you?"

He smiled, feeling foolish. "I wasn't sure and I wouldn't have blamed you in the least, it was stupid. Am I forgiven?"

Janet, sitting on the other side of Maxie, couldn't help but hear their conversation. She kept her eyes averted, looking instead at the feet in the pool. Old feet are not pretty, she concluded, and wanted to pull hers out and put her shoes back on. But the water felt too good.

Buddy sat on the curve of the pool facing them. Soon Dee came out of the house. He smiled as she came over to sit down next to him, relieved that she was at least joining in.

"Is everyone cooling off?" He listened to their comments and continued. "Let's get started then." Reaching into the folder he was holding, he held up a long piece of paper. "This is our announcements and I think they look great," he said scanning the paper. He looked at Jake. "You did a great job Jake," then quickly added, "and you too of course Mildred."

Jake nodded his head in thanks.

"Jake did most of the work on that Buddy," demurred Mildred.

"Well hardly, the machines... "

"Not really," interrupted Mildred.

Buddy didn't have time for this you did he did shit. "Okay, okay, you both did a great job, now lets..." "

Before he could finish, Gus came strolling out of the house. He walked down the steps and over to the pool where most of them were sitting. He unzipped his pants and peed. The long, strong stream going into the water between their feet.

Leon was the first to jerk his feet out of the water. The others too stunned to move. "Gus, for Christ sakes! What the hell are you doing?"

"Gus!" Buddy sprang up and walked quickly to Gus's side, wanting to push the son of a bitch into the pool.

It was the final straw for Dee. She sat stupidly pointing at the cute decorative sign on the fence that read: "PLEASE DON'T PEE IN THE POOL, THE WATER I DRINK MIGHT BE YOURS!" "Buddeeeee!" she screeched.

Janet had been too fascinated to move. You could say she had a dog's eye view, as Gus was standing almost over her feet at the pool's edge. She could actually feel the warmth as the heat of the urine mixed with the cool water.

The size of Gus's penis dumbfounded her, since her only means of comparison had been Andrew. She thought they must all be like short stubby pencils.

Now, sitting with what felt like a water balloon between her legs, she felt a stirring of pleasure as she moved slightly to avoid getting wet.

Jake made an attempt to get up succeeding only on the second try. "My God man, what's wrong with you?" he demanded.

Gus paid no attention to any of them. He zipped up his pants, turned and walked back towards the house.

They watched him walk back up the stairs. "Is he still asleep? He looked like he was still asleep," insisted Mildred.

"Bull Shit," Leon spat out, outraged. "He did that deliberately. I just know it."

The phrase made Jake stop and look at Leon. "Wait a minute," he said, suddenly remembering a similar scene years ago at Spinning during a practice. A bunch of guys were just sitting around the pool when this guy did the same thing. He was trying to be funny and deliberately urinated into the pool, splashing some of the swimmers in the process. He could actually see the event in his mind, but not the young man.

"What's the matter?" asked Leon.

Jake told them the story, then looked over at Buddy. "You were there too, Buddy. I'm pretty sure of it."

Buddy had been remembering it too. It brought back the same memories only he knew who it was. "I'll be damned,

80

Merlin August," he said mostly to himself, but loud enough to be overheard.

"Right!" said Jake. "That's right, Merlin August."

"Who, what did you say?" asked Mildred.

"Could Gus be Merlin August, Jake?" Buddy asked in a strange voice.

"Who's Merlin August?" Janet and Maxie asked at the same time.

"Is that possible?" asked Leon ignoring their question. "I thought he died or had gone to prison or something."

Dee was keenly listening and noticed Buddy had become very quiet. "Buddy?" said Dee.

Soon all eyes were on him. "I really didn't know who he was when he cornered me at the store a few months back. He certainly doesn't look anything like the Merlin August I remember, that's for sure," he explained. "He said he had gone to Spinning and graduated in '46.

He knew a lot about Dee and me and about a lot of the people in our class. He said his name was Gus Randolf." Buddy looked from one to the other. "I thought he was probably in the January class and didn't really think any more about it."

"You didn't mention that to me before," said Dee, a deep frown creasing her brow.

Buddy was starting to feel a little uncomfortable under her gaze, and he could tell she clearly had more questions to ask him.

"Well," he said licking his lips. "Like I said, I thought he was from the January class, but he wasn't anything like he is now, I'll bet he put on thirty pounds since I saw him."

He was talking fast, too fast. He tried to slow down. "I like a jerk, mentioned I was going to get a committee together for our 50th," he ended lamely, seeing the fury in Dee's eyes.

"You mean you're responsible for that man being on our committee?" she asked incredulously. "You said you didn't remember how he got wind of it," she lashed out at him.

A path cleared as she moved with great speed on her size fours towards the already cowering Buddy. The other committee members clustered in little groups at the edge of the pool.

"Well, I didn't exactly ask him, you know...he just sort of volunteered, "he offered.

"For Christ's sake Buddy!" she yelled, forgetting they were not alone.

"What was I supposed to do...tell him he couldn't come?..Like hell!" he shouted back, finally getting angry.

"Hey Guys, guys. Come one," Leon said trying to get between them to calm them down.

Dee shoved him aside as if he were a beach ball, and continued to berate her husband.

"Now just a Goddamn minute little lady," said an outraged Leon, as he stumbled backwards, bumping into Mildred who happened to be standing with her back to the edge of the pool, and they could only go one way.

Mildred was hollering something like, "My hair!" as they tumbled sideways into the pool.

Leon began flailing his arms about and sputtering, "Help, I can't," before grabbing Mildred around the neck, causing them both to sink.

Janet watched all the splashing, then realized Leon, and for that matter Mildred, were both in trouble.

Without another thought she jumped in feet first, causing her long full skirt to spread out around her, completely engulfing her head as she came up for air.

She grabbed at the skirt, trying to bring it down around her knees. She had seen no need to wear a slip on such a hot day, only her Depends, never dreaming of course, she would be in such a predicament. The undergarment began filling with water immediately, feeling like a bag of wet cement, pulling her down.

Maxie and Jake rushed over to the edge, across from where Leon and Mildred were struggling. Somehow they were in the middle and at the deep end. Mildred was trying to get Leon to let go of her. Even though she had been a good swimmer in her younger days, in his panic Leon was just too strong for her and she was getting tired.

"Jake, we have to do something!" yelled Maxie, as she began throwing everything that would float into the pool, including some things that wouldn't.

The hosts were so wrapped up in their arguing they failed to notice the seriousness of things going on around them.

"Dammit, you two, quit that and get over here!" hollered Jake, making an effort to help Maxie.

It was Mildred's last effort, a scream that finally got Buddy and Dee's attention. They immediately rushed to help, a fleeting thought of lawsuits flashing in their minds.

Buddy, dressed in shorts dove in, swimming quickly to Mildred's aid. "Stop it Leon," Buddy told a wild eyed and thrashing Leon. "I've got you." He grabbed at Leon's belt and pulled him away from Mildred and towards the edge. "Relax. Relax, I won't let you go," he kept repeating, until he had Leon close enough to the edge so he could grab hold. Buddy turned to see Mildred swimming for the steps, then pulled himself out so he could help Leon.

Janet, however, was having some difficulty with buoyancy, and felt herself beginning to sink. Or so she thought. Hating to give up her secret, she had no choice but to undo the Velcro tabs on each side and let the Depends sink, float, or whatever. Maybe with all the cushions and all the other stuff she saw floating, no one would notice. All she could do was hope. Her immediate problem was getting out of the pool now that she had seen Buddy save Mildred.

When she swam to the edge and tried to hang on to the ladder, her skirt floated on top of the water, exposing her nakedness underneath. Looking up she noticed two size four's with toenails painted bright red and Dee looking down, a puzzled expression on her face.

"Janet, are you okay?"

Trying to push her skirt down with one hand, she could only sputter, "I think so."

Dee let out a little shriek. "My God Janet, you don't have anything on!"

Angry and tired, Janet exploded. "For Christ's sake Dee, get a damn towel and help me!"

Shocked at her language, Dee just stood there until Janet's free hand whacked at her foot with a quick chop, getting her attention.

Slightly limping, Dee moved quickly gathering a towel from off one of the chaises and rushed back to help Janet.

Too mad now to care how much was exposed, Janet climbed the ladder and wrapped herself with the towel Dee held out for her. She noticed no one else was paying attention to her anyway. The rest were trying to save Leon, who was still protesting between coughs.

Mildred sat on a chair, looking like a skinned rat. Finding a towel, she tightly wrapped herself in it, too exhausted to do anything else, except think. Leon the fool, almost killed her. What would have happened to Ma. She shivered.

No one noticed Gus.

He was standing just inside the glass doors, looking down at the pool. He watched as Leon and Mildred struggled with each other. He saw Janet. He really saw Janet.

If Gus had known he was responsible for all the madness, he would certainly have taken pleasure from it. But he had only just awakened a few moments before from his trance-like sleep, standing there by the glass doors.

He turned and went back to the family room. "Ninety-five-twenty-five them all," he said stooping to pick up the large box containing the announcements he had seen Jake put down earlier on the coffee table. He made his way to the front door and out.

The class of 1946 of dear old Spinning High would soon hear from Merlin August, after almost 50 years.

Leon, finally out of the water, lay exhausted on his back at the edge of the pool. Spasms of choking, coughing and spitting up the water from the pool, made him roll over onto his side.

He was dangerously close to the edge. Unfortunately, when no one was standing near enough, a new spasm started. Over onto his side he rolled, but this time right back into the pool.

Buddy had gone behind one of the large trees to check his toupee for some needed adjustment, since Leon almost pulled it off.

Being the closest, Jake had no choice but to jump in and help Leon, who seemed to have lost his will to live, for he no longer thrashed about, only sank like a stone.

Retrieving Leon again, they insisted he lay on the only chaise pad left, far away from the edge of the pool.

The only two who weren't wet had been busy. Maxie, in the midst of all the turmoil, didn't have time to think about anything except throwing things in the pool, and helping Dee round up towels. She certainly didn't notice that Dee hadn't said a word as she grabbed another towel and threw it across Jake's shoulders.

Dee was livid. If she had wanted a swim party, she would have sent out cute little announcements. She looked around at her soggy, so called friends. Her pool was a mess. Everything was either floating or lying on the bottom. Two chaise pads were ruined, thanks to Maxie. Couldn't she see those were not the floating kind. Not only did Gus pee in there, but also she spotted what appeared to be a large diaper.

When she saw what looked to be a long turd floating on the water, her knees caved in. My God, she thought, we'll have to drain and disinfect the pool. Even when she realized it was only one of Leon's cigars, she found it to be almost as offensive.

When her services were no longer needed, she went back into the house, intending to gather up everyone's belongings and bring them outside. No way were any of them going to drip all over her carpets. The ingrates!

While she was gathering the stuff, Buddy came in wrapped in a large print pool towel. "You okay hon?" he asked timidly. He had seen her expression out there and knew something was up.

"You'd better not be dripping," she said accusingly.

"No, I took care of it. "See, I got the towel."

"I want those people out of here," she said pointing in the direction of the pool. "Look what they've done to the pool. They hated my surprise. They just don't appreciate anything

I...we, try to do." She threw her hands in the air. "The hell with them. And another thing, that Gus..."

Before she could finish, Buddy said, "Where is Gus, by the way?" They both looked around.

Immediately Dee got panicky. "My God, I hope he's not laying down somewhere, like on our bed. I couldn't stand that Buddy." She headed for the bedroom with Buddy right behind.

The room was empty. "Oh thank God," she said.

"Let me go look for his car, see if it's gone," he said as he rushed out of the room to look out a window facing the street. "It's okay, he's gone," he called out.

"Oh Buddy, you know just the thought of him laying on anything in this house, gives me the willies. I just can't stand it."

A few moments later she found Buddy standing in the family room looking down at the coffee table with a frown on his face.

"Buddy?" she asked, walking into the room. "What's wrong? What is it?"

"That box that Jake brought, he put it on this table, didn't he?"

She nodded her head. "I'm pretty sure."

They glanced around the room checking other tables and chairs, even looking on the floor. "It's not here," he said.

Their nemesis had struck again. "Gus! they said looking at each other.

AFTER:

On the way home in Maxie's car, Mildred and Janet sat quietly on pieces of plastic that Buddy dug up for them. Their clothing was no longer dripping, the heat had taken care of that, but they were damp and uncomfortable.

Both of them were worn out after their ordeals, and Maxie relished the quiet. The headache was starting again.

It was strange, she thought, the way Dee rushed them out of the backyard as if to say, "Here's you're hat, what's you're hurry." Bringing our purses and stuff out of the house like that. Strange. The whole thing was a fiasco from start to finish. That stupid mirrored ball. God, what was she thinking? Nothing was accomplished come to think of it. We just spent all our time fishing people out of that pool.

Smiling she thought of Jake, of what a really nice guy he was. Jumping in after Leon that second time. That poor Leon, he's helpless, helpless. Again Mickey Mouse popped into her head. Wonder what he's like at home, and his wife, wonder what she has to put up with?

Mildred sniffed, interrupting her thoughts. Maxie looked over and felt a great surge of affection for her. Poor Millie, it must have been terrible for her in that pool. My gosh. It suddenly hit her how close they had come to having a real tragedy today. She looked in the rearview mirror at Janet, quiet and bedraggled, and felt a rush of fondness for her two friends.

Maxie rubbed her temple thinking about Dee. Boy, she was really pissed. I'm sure mostly at me. I ruined her little dumb surprise. Maxie sighed. How were we supposed to see each other or take notes if necessary? Not that we've had anything to take notes on so far. Oh the hell with it, she thought. She was anxious to talk to Jake.

Janet was studying the back of Maxie and Mildred's heads, but her thoughts were back at the pool. She hadn't had too much time to think about Gus after the initial shock of seeing him so up close and personal like that. Even now her eyes opened wide at the thought of him.

Everything was sticking to her making her miserable and uncomfortable. She could hardly wait to get out of her clothes. Dee rushed them out so fast, she didn't even get a chance to use the bathroom. To her everlasting shame, the Depends didn't sink, but she saw it rippling merrily on top of the water.

The damp tight frizz was plastered to Mildred's scull. I didn't help her, Janet thought, feeling guilty. I did jump in with good intentions, but I was so worried about sinking and my skirt and my, she winced, nakedness.

She didn't want to think about that now. The Godman would have had a stroke if he'd seen me. I guess I can be thankful for that at least. Suddenly her eyes widened again, her thoughts had gone back to Gus.

Mildred couldn't forget that feeling of helplessness in the water. Not being able to get away from Leon. The crazy old fool, how come he never learned how to swim, she wondered. She could still feel the water stealing her breath away and the way her chest felt like it would explode.

Mildred let out a gasp as she tried to move her neck. Then realized she was sore all over. She shuddered remembering the terror in his eyes. He was so powerful and had such a tight grip on her. I wonder what my eyes looked like to him, she thought.

And Ma. She thought of Ma when she was in the water, not herself really. What if something really happened, Ma would have to go live with her brother Jim in Tennessee.

Jim's okay, she told herself, but he knows nothing about doing for Ma. All her doctors are here. She'd die quicker without me, I'm sure. Besides, he wouldn't have patience with her and her problems. She shivered in the heat. That wife of his would want to put Ma in a home. I never liked Gloria, she told herself.

Why did it take so long for anybody to help me? She sniffled again, loudly. What were they doing while I was fighting for my life. Mildred looked sideways at Maxie. She's certainly not wet, is she, she noticed.

Things started to look fuzzy. Putting her hand to her eyes she asked, "My glasses, where are my glasses?"

"Are they in you're purse?" asked Maxie.

Mildred picked up her purse and rummaged through it. "Just my case is here."

"Did you have them on when you fell in the pool? Do you remember?"

"Of course I remember!" Mildred was angry. She threw her purse down on the floor by her feet. "I'm not always out of it, you know. I do remember some things!"

"Mildred, I'm sorry, what's wrong?" Maxie apologized even though she didn't understand why.

Letting the real reason for her anger surface, she asked, "Why did it take so long for any of you to help me?" and burst into tears.

Janet leaned forward touching Mildred's shoulder.

"I did jump in Millie, as soon as I saw you were in trouble. My skirt kept dragging me down, as well as other things," she added, not wanting to go into it if she didn't have to. "I really tried to get to you dear, honest."

Painfully, Mildred turned to face Janet, tears streaming down her face. "Really?"

"Really," said Maxie, reaching across the seat and touching Mildred's arm. "Jake and I were throwing everything we could find into the pool for Leon to grab hold of. Janet jumped right in, then Buddy..." She didn't want to tell her that Buddy and Dee were arguing, not paying any attention, Mildred didn't need to hear that now. "Buddy jumped in and fought with Leon, trying to get him off of you," she added. "He was just crazed."

Mildred was nodding her head. "I know, I saw it in his eyes. He was so afraid." "It's over now Mil," Maxie said softly.

Janet gave Mildred a reassuring pat on her shoulder.

"You know, after Leon let go, I was so tired I could hardly make it over to the steps." Actually, she couldn't remember where she was for a moment, but she didn't want to tell them that, or the fact that she didn't remember how she got out of the pool.

"But you did. You did," said Maxie, handing over a box of tissues to her friend.

Janet slid back on the plastic where a new puddle was quickly absorbed by her damp skirt.

* * * *

Leon's brain was numb as he drove slowly, not trusting his reflexes. The heat in the car did nothing to stop the numbing cold that went right to his bones. He couldn't stop shaking as he reached a trembling hand up to his chest. He was sure there was a pocket there. He felt around but it was gone. Slowly looking down at the ripped spot where the pocket had been, he tried to remember why he needed one.

Moments of confusion engulfed him before he recalled he and Mildred thrashing around in the pool. "My God, my God, he repeated over and over until the memory faded and the confusion returned.

Only Leon's instinct and a strong habit made him reach for a cigar, only he couldn't remember how or where to get one. Squinting from the glare of the sun, he put a shaky hand up to shield his eyes, forgetting the car had a visor.

Stabbing pains shot through his feet and up his skinny legs. He wept in his helplessness needing Martha. He just wanted to make it home to Martha. She'd know what to do.

Driving slowly, practically at a crawl, he stayed close to the right hand side. Only through sheer luck, did Leon avoid any parked cars in his path. Another sight flashed in his mind.

"Son of a Bitch!" he yelled, remembering who had maliciously pushed him into that death trap. Feeling a surge of anger and an amazing burst of strength, his foot pressed down on the gas pedal while he looked around for something to punch at.

It was the last thing he remembered as his car plowed into the back of the pick up truck in front of him.

The driver, young, large and muscular, angrily got out of his truck. Forgotten for the moment the call he had just received from his radio dispatcher to clean out a pool's circulation system, recently plugged with a variety of objects.

Muttering obscenities as he strode back to check out the damage, he found a dazed Leon, gone back into shock.

* * * *

"The pool man should be here pretty soon," Buddy said putting down the cordless phone. He looked sideways at Dee. She was lying on the only chaise left in tact, staring straight ahead, not saying a word. He knew from past experience that it was a bad, bad sign.

"We can replace anything that's ruined, hon," he added, trying to get some reaction from her. Shaking his head, he looked at the mess in the pool. Might as well get it over with he decided. She kept staring." I know it didn't go too well today..."

That got a reaction, "Go to well, you mean it went to hell!" she screamed suddenly, sitting up and turning all her anger towards him. Shrinking visibly he wanted to cover his ears.

"This was the worst day of my life!" Her chin jutted out and her fists were clenched. He moved away from her. "That's it! I do not want any of those ingrates, ever," she emphasized, "back in this house...ever!"

Buddy blinked. "But hon, the reunion. What about the..."

"Never mind," she interrupted. "We'll start a new committee, with new people." She glared at him. "We've got the list. We, we"... she paused. "We can start fresh." The idea appealed to her and a look of hope crossed her face.

Buddy paled. "Sweet Jesus," he muttered.

"No, now think about it." Her look was as eager as a kid in a toy store. "We won't have to put up with that maniac Gus any longer. Wouldn't that be wonderful, you know he's always ruining our meetings," she finished smugly. She waited for him to agree with her.

She's actually smiling he noticed. My God, she thinks she has the answer. This is a nightmare, how am I going to tell her?

Dee still wasn't finished. "And Leon, thank goodness no more cigars!" She eyed the pool distastefully. "Buddy," she said getting up and pointing her finger at him. "We have to make sure none of the new men smoke those awful cigars." Buddy rolled his eyes heavenward.

"And Janet!" her eyes glittered. "Did you see what she did?"

"What's wrong with Janet? You're not still upset about her spilling that drink the last time, are you?" he asked, going along with her, prolonging the inevitable.

"That...no, this is worse. She swore at me...she's a minister's wife, for God's sake!" she exclaimed, highly insulted. "And, she wears some kind of a diaper." She folded her arms across her chest. Dee was enjoying herself, loving the gossip. "Didn't you see it in the pool? She was actually naked from the waist down!" She paused dramatically. "I saw her Buddy, when she was climbing the ladder, trying to get out."

"Janet?" he was incredulous. "But, she's..."

Malice burned brightly in Dee's eyes. "Exactly..Janet!"

She still wasn't finished. "Maxie! Did you see what she did?"

"But Maxie's you're best friend."

"Not anymore, she's not! She didn't like my mirrored ball!" she said angrily. "It was a great idea, and she made me look like a fool. I just wanted everyone to have some fun," she said feeling sorry for herself.

"Sweetheart, you're just upset now." He wondered if he should go to her, touch her, try to hug her. He nixed that, remembering other times and her bony fist. Forget it, once he couldn't go out without his dark glasses for a whole week, just because he forgot to duck. "Wait till you have a chance to think about everything. We'll find a way to sort this out." He was trying optimism he didn't feel.

"No way!" she said over her shoulder, heading for the house.

"Where are you going?" he asked anxiously close at her heels.

"I am going to get the other list. We'll go through it and pick a new committee. Simple!"

She opened the sliding glass door and walked inside.

"No wait!" He followed her into the house. Right now, he decided, he'd rather be facing a root canal. "Dee, ah, ah.. we can't."

"I've made up my mind Buddy. That's all there is to it! Since none of them appreciated all the things I've done, ah, we've done for them. Well, we don't need them. We don't need any of them." She headed down the hall towards the den. "Come on, I want to get started on this. Now, where's the original list?"

His heart gave a sickening lurch. "There isn't any." He grabbed his chest, waiting. Now Lord, take me now, before I have to explain, he prayed.

She stopped in mid-stride. "What?" She turned around facing him.

He was sure he felt the walls reverberate. "I'm sorry hon, but there is no original." He shut his eyes and scrunched up his face. "Gus has it..."

"You gave Gus our original?"

"No, not exactly. I... ah, there never was an original, just a copy.

"That was the only one, and...Gus has it," he added weakly, opening his eyes slowly but keeping his face scrunched.

He braced himself against the wall, waiting for the explosion that was sure to follow.

But, she only stood there, looking at him with a slightly dazed expression. "Honey?" he asked.

Dee crumpled, right before his eyes.

* * * *

"I'll come right down," Martha said, putting down the phone and grabbing her purse.

Arriving at the hospital, she found a pale and shaken Leon, covered with blankets up to his nose.

"Martha, Martha, thank God you've come," he blubbered weakly at the sight of her. "Today, Martha, you almost lost me, you almost lost your dear husband today." He grabbed for the hand she held out to him, knocking the blankets off.

Noticing the wide plastic collar around his neck, she asked worriedly, "Leon, what happened? They said you were in an accident, What kind?" she rearranged the blankets around his shoulders.

"You name it!" he said in a stronger voice. Then reverting back to the pathetic, added, "Two, Martha, I was in two!" He tried to show her two fingers but the blanket got in the way so he let his hand drop down helplessly.

"How?" she asked, picking up and stroking his hand.

"It was terrible, terrible. I think I almost drowned." He was trying to move his head from side to side for emphasis, with little success.

"And they tell me I ran into a car." He waited until she pulled the blankets back up to his chin. "But that I'm kinda fuzzy on." He pulled the blanket part way off his chest. "Look Martha, my shirt, ruined," he sighed. "My glasses too... probably in that hell hole pool, I'll bet" He was getting agitated.

"It's okay Leon, calm down," she said soothingly. "Don't worry about the shirt or your glasses, they can be replaced. But you can't my dear, I'm just glad you're alright." She ran her fingers gently through his thick damp hair, softly stroking his worried brow and he lapped it up.

Martha was here. He closed his eyes in agreement and let out a big sigh.

"Tsk, tsk," he sighed again. "You're right Martha, you're right. I should get right down on my knees and give thanks," he said reaching for the blankets, his voice very weak.

"Not now Leon, not now!" She pulled the blankets up again. "Are you hurt anywhere? Have you seen a doctor yet?" she asked looking around.

"Just some damn kid and a nurse." he said loudly.

"Sh, Leon!"

"Well, he sure didn't do much, and my chest is sore. I swallowed a hell of a lot of that pool. And I think my neck hurt before." He gave her a soulful look. "But I think I'm okay," he said grimacing.

"Then why are you making that face then? Are you in pain now?" she asked worriedly.

"My feet, they really hurt, can you take my shoes off Martha, I can't stand it they feel so cramped."

Martha leaned over and removed his shoes, but while taking the left one off, a sock came out stuck between his toes.

She laughed. "Here's you're problem Leon." She held up the socks for him to see. "You forgot to take them out of your shoes." She didn't ask him why he put them there.

He barely noticed. Wiggling his little fat toes, a look of pure bliss on his face.

It didn't last long however, as Martha looked down into those sad runny eyes he told her about his miserable day, but in spurts, only the parts he remembered, starting with Dee's mirrored ball. "You should have seen it Martha, it would have made you puke."

She listened quietly, asking only one question when he finished. "So tell me, how did you get into that pool again?"

Before he could answer, a young man in white came in saying he was from X-ray and told them he was taking Leon downstairs.

As he was being wheeled out, Martha heard his voice. This time stronger, much stronger.

"I was pushed, Goddamn it!" he bellowed. "I was pushed!"

* * * *

Gus stacked the announcements into a neat pile. He picked them up, banged the edges on the desk making sure they were neatly squared off. Putting them down next to the stacks of envelopes, he accidentally moved one envelope out of line. Picking up that stack, he banged them on the edge making sure they were neatly squared, then laid them down.

Gus surveyed the top of his desk. A smile, looking more like a leer, slashed his face. He had it all. He was totally in control now and he knew it. This was his fee-ucking ball game, and soon they would all know it.

His glance rested on the list, protected in a clear plastic folder against any accidents involving liquid of any kind.

Unexpectedly his knees gave out and he had to grab hold of the edge of the desk to keep from falling. The exhaustion he felt startled him. Earlier, when he found himself standing by the glass doors, he felt wonderful, as if he'd had a good night's sleep. The feeling had stayed with him until now.

Taking small unsteady steps, he moved slowly towards the only chair in the sparsely furnished room, the one behind the desk. Sitting down heavily, he leaned backwards closing his eyes in weariness.

Trying to recall the afternoon was difficult for Gus. He remembered walking into that fee-ucking room. Then what, he wondered. The lights...that fee-ucking ball shooting lights all over the fee-ucking room. Try as he might, that's all he could remember, until he was standing by those fee-ucking doors. What the fee-uck happened, he asked himself, then realized something else was wrong.

Why was he saying that word to himself, instead of the number? That crazy broad did something to my fee-ucking head. He grabbed a pen, held it over a piece of paper and waited for his mind to clear, to remember...what? "The fee-ucking number!" he shouted. "That piss-ant took my fee-ucking number!"

He grasped an envelope. There, typed on the bottom left hand corner; 9525. He flipped the envelope over. On the flap was 5952 with slashes across the numbers and 9525 typed below it.

"Nine, five, two, five, that's it!" he sighed. "That's 9525ing it!"

But the lost afternoon still troubled him until he remembered going with the wife to the circus years ago. They had one of those 9525-ing balls there, too. The wife had to wake him up. Told him he slept through the whole 9525-ing circus.

I wonder what happened today while I wasn't there? he asked himself. He didn't like the idea that things went on and he didn't know about it, he didn't like that a bit.

For the briefest moment, normal curiosity overcame him. What were Leon and that prissy schoolteacher doing in the pool? Looked like they were fighting, and what's her name...the one whose ass was blowing in the breeze? She was in the pool too.

She's some 9525-ing preacher's wife, ain't she? He chuckled mulling over that picture for a bit. Come to think of it, and he hadn't for years and years, it wasn't too bad. A little broad, but he liked it that way.

He almost felt sorry he missed all the fun and wondered how it started until another part of his brain took over and told him he didn't give a 9525.

His only interest at the moment was his special surprise for all of them. The 9525-ing committee and his 9525-ing classmates. That's all he cared about, it's what consumed him, after all, he had been waiting 50 years for this. He rubbed his stubble head back and forth deep in thought, imagining his sweet revenge.

* * * *

Heading home in his car, a soggy Jake, said the two names outloud. "Merlin August, Gus Randolf." He shook his head in wonderment. Something's wrong here, he told himself. This meeting was the worst yet. If he hadn't seen it with his own eyes he wouldn't have believed it. Anxious to talk to Maxie about it, he wondered if she was home yet.

He was glad to get home, his clothes were starting to chafe his skin. First, he told himself, I'm going to have to peel everything off.

Undressing, he reached back to get his wallet out of his pants pocket. Carefully pulling the pictures apart in their plastic covers and was pleased to see they were hardly wet.

Checking Fran's picture, he sighed in relief. It was okay, that's all that mattered. He had carried that particular picture around for years, it was his favorite. He studied it for a moment remembering exactly when it was taken.

They were at the beach, her hair looked golden in the bright sun as she smiled into the camera waving at him. He smiled back.

In the bathroom, he laid out cards and money to dry on the countertop. "Not too bad," he muttered.

The phone rang as he was stepping out of the shower. Grabbing a towel he raced towards the bedroom. "Hello," he said picking it up.

"Jake? It's Maxie."

"Hi" he smiled into the phone. "I was just thinking about you."

Smiling, she warmed to his voice. "Is this a bad time?"

Dripping, he tried drying himself while holding the phone to his ear and shoulder, doing a balancing act. He realized he was not as agile as he once was when the towel fell to the floor and the phone slipped from his wet shoulder.

Maxie waited for a response. "Jake? You okay?"

"Yeah, sure," he laughed. "Almost dropped the phone. I just stepped out of the shower and I'm dripping. Where are you when I need to be dried off…."

He heard a sound on the other end and wasn't sure what it was. Being from the old school, he suddenly realized how risqué' that sounded. "My Gosh. Sorry, I was just referring to...ah, I was just thinking about you giving me that towel today." He waited to see if she was going to hang up. "Maxie?" Her laughter exploded in his ear.

"I hope you didn't pinch yourself again, while I'm making a complete ass of myself," he scolded playfully. Just then he saw himself in the full-length mirror on the closet door.

Wrinkled ass, he amended, looking at himself. Who was that stooped old man with the gray hair? Strange, when he talked to Maxie he felt younger, stronger. It really came as a shock and he was lost for a moment in disappointment, wishing he looked more like his former self. He pried his eyes away from the sorry sight and concentrated on Maxie's voice.

"Jake, Jake, it's okay. Don't apologize." She was still laughing, trying to picture the scene. "Why don't you finish up and give me a call back, okay?"

"Okay," he said relieved. "It seems I can only manage one thing at a time. I'll call you right back." He threw her a kiss, making the sound before he could stop himself. He hung up quickly.

Whenever he said goodbye to Fran on the phone, he always did that. It was just a natural reflex, what else. Or was it? He grinned knowing he couldn't take it back and knowing hey, he didn't want to.

When he finished dressing he sat down on the bed and called her back.

"Hi Jake," she answered on the first ring.

He listened for anything different in her voice. It seemed okay. "Hi, Maxie." He felt suddenly shy.

"Jake?" she paused. "Did I hear a kiss before you hung up?"

"Did you mind?" he held his breath.

"I liked it...a lot."

He was smiling and breathing. At that moment he decided to get expensive tennis shoes, join a health club and get back in shape. At least better shape. He hoped it wasn't too late. They both started talking at the same time, then stopped. "You first," Jake said.

"Okay. Well, I wanted to talk about today. It gets stranger and stranger, but can it get any worse?"

"Who knows? But it's hard to imagine that it can. Do you remember Merlin August?" he asked.

There was a moment's silence. "No, I'm sure I don't. Who or where did he come from?"

"No doubt about it, he really was in our class, but I don't think he graduated with the rest of us. I haven't looked in the yearbook yet, but I will later," Jake said. "The thing that gets me, is him palming himself off as Gus Randolf. Why? Why the deception?"

"He's scary and so intense. What do you think he really wants? Why is he even on the committee, he's not the least bit sociable?" Maxie asked.

Jake stretched himself out on the bed, adjusting the pillows under his head, making himself comfortable. "That Maxie, is the sixty-four dollar question."

"Also, Jake, I forgot to ask you how you felt after you're swim today?" Maxie pulled her robe tighter around her, tucking her feet under her, settling into the corner of the couch. She laughed. "Just about everyone was in the pool at one time or another, except Dee and myself."

"You missed out, the water was great. Too bad I wasn't dressed for it." He laughed at the thought. "I even surprised myself, jumping in like that. But I had to. That poor devil Leon. Imagine, falling in twice." They laughed a little self-consciously. "I did ask him if he wanted a ride home, but he said he was okay," Jake said. "I hope he made it home in one piece." Neither mentioned Gus peeing in the pool.

"For awhile, it was really serious, wasn't it?" she asked.

"That's for sure. I think we were all lucky that nothing more serious happened. By the way, how's Millie?" he asked as if suddenly remembering.

"She was so upset on the way home. Oh Jake, you should have heard her." Maxie wanted to cry just thinking about it. "She wondered why it took so long for someone to help her. Leon was pulling her under and she couldn't get away from him."

"Poor Millie," Jake said.

"It must have been so terrifying for her. She was crying, Jake," she said with concern.

"Gus!" he spat out. "That son of a bitch! It always seems to start with him. Excuse my language."

"You're excused. Do you think he was really asleep out there, like Millie said?" she asked.

"I think he's a devious bastard, awake or asleep."

* * * *

Mildred was so tired. She ached all over. All she wanted was to get home, get out of her damp clothes, they felt like they weighed a ton. The ride seemed to take forever. Thank goodness she picked me up today, she thought, glancing over at Maxie. She knew by the way she felt, she couldn't have driven home.

She was grateful to be let off at her front door, and gave a quick wave, not looking to see if they waved back as she went into the house.

"Ma, I'm home," she said in a relieved voice. Wanting to cry for some reason, she kept blinking back tears.

Angie, who had been sitting with Bella, came out of the front room. Her smile faded when she noticed Mildred's condition, her damp wrinkled clothes, not to mention how pale she was.

"What happened Millie?" she asked moving towards her.

Mildred grabbed her arm, pulling her into the kitchen. "Sh!, I don't want to upset Ma," but then she succumbed to Angie's look of concern, her kindness, and burst into tears again. "Millerd?" Ma's little voice called out.

"Just a minute Bella, we'll be right there," said Angie.

With Angie's arms around her she started to get that closed in feeling she had in the pool. "It's okay Angie," she said trying to untangle herself out of Angie's arms. "Just give me a minute."

Calming down a bit, she walked into the front room. Ma started to laugh thinking it was some kind of joke. "Millerd, what happened?" she said between cackles. "Look you're hair, you wet?"

"Long story, Ma." Then laughter and tears mixed together. Ma's laugh always did get to her.

Between spasm's of laughter and wiping away the tears that flowed down her cheeks, Mildred told them of her ordeal.

Bella stopped laughing. Angie became even more concerned.

101

* * * *

Hanging up the phone, Maxie lay her head back against the pillows with her eyes closed. Her thoughts on Jake, going over the conversation she just had with him.

A smile crossed her face. Jake, that shy, sweet man had actually thrown her a kiss. She sat up suddenly. It was just probably something he always did with Fran, a habit that just happened, she scolded herself. Her smile faded, but then she relaxed again and leaned back. No, he admitted it, so it must have been for her personally.

Getting up, she went down the hall to her bedroom. Jake would be picking her up soon, she had to decide what to wear.

She didn't ordinarily like to look at her body, but taking off her robe she deliberately looked at herself in the large mirror over her dresser, trying to see herself through someone else's eyes...like Jake's.

Posing, turning this way and that only brought on anxieties. She held in her stomach, raised her arms. That wasn't too bad that way she thought, but who walks around with their arms in the air?

With the lowering of her arms the transformations was to say the least, a catastrophe. "Forget it, no one is going to see me naked!" she said to the woman in the mirror.

Sitting in an office all day long did nothing to keep her in shape. True, she was still slim enough, but slim without firm was still no great shakes, she noted. How the heck did all that sagging and drooping occur without her noticing it?

She was just turning sideways, checking herself out to see if there was suddenly a miraculous change, when Jeezer flung open her bedroom door

"Gram! Oh, man, fuck...oh man," he repeated, rooted to the spot.

She could only stare at him, like a deer caught in the headlights of an oncoming car.

She waited for him to cover his eyes or turn away, but he did neither. The only movement he made was to push his still blue tinged bangs out of his eyes with a furious motion as if to make sure he saw what he saw.

Maxie, for lack of imagination and totally speechless, stepped over to the closet door, opened it, stepped inside and closed the door.

The quiet was disturbing.

"Jeezer?" she finally called from the closet.

"Yeah?"

"You still out there?"

"Yeah," he said.

She waited. "Well, would you get the hell out!"

"Oh, man...yeah."

Maxie waited again to hear the sound of the door closing, but there was none.

"NOW!" she screamed.

This time she heard the door slam.

Opening the closet door a tiny crack, she peered out. He was gone. Rigid with indignation, she wondered what was the matter with Carrie? Didn't she ever teach the kid to knock? She had to blame somebody for this, and logically at that moment, it had to be her daughter as she walked over to the door and locked it.

Feeling a bit guilty for her thoughts, she realized it was her own fault. That's what locks are for, idiot! she told herself.

"Now what am I going to do?" she asked herself looking in the mirror. Visualizing all those sneery little looks she would probably get from those pimply face friends of his, she snatched up her robe and covered herself.

"Dammit, now I'm gonna have to join the Foreign Legion" she said walking into the bathroom and locking the door behind her.

* * * *

"Honey?"

Dee sat on the floor in the hall. Her legs spread out in front of her, her head forward down near her knees.

103

"Honey, Dee, are you okay?" Buddy knelt down by her side. Dee didn't move.

"Dee, you're scaring me. Say something please!" he begged.

"It's all ruined. All my plans are ruined." She said it in a monotone, over and over like a mantra, while her head bobbed up and down.

"We don't know that, hon. Really." He patted her shoulder, then stroked her hair. "I'll call Gus," he said in desperation. "I'll see if we can get the list back."

She stopped bobbing and turned her head to look up at him. "How can you? I thought you didn't know how to get in touch with him." Her eyes narrowed. "He always called you, you said."

"I know, we don't have an address, but I do have a phone number remember? Come on, let me help you up," he said standing up and holding his arms out to her.

She lifted her head while moving her legs under her, then held up her arms to him.

"I don't want to work with him ever again, Buddy," she said in a small voice as he pulled her up.

"Neither do I hon, Jeeze, neither do I!"

Dee followed him into the study. The oversized desk and chair took up three fourths of the small room. It was the only thing Buddy had that once belonged to his father, and it was his greatest treasure.

The walls, paneled in a deep walnut, did not fight the carpeting for a change. Since Dee had very little to do with it, it was the nicest room in the house.

She stood by his side as Buddy took the chair behind the desk. Luckily, there was a foot ring about a foot up around the base of the chair. Otherwise, Buddy's feet no doubt would be dangling.

Dee watched impatiently as Buddy looked up Gus's number and dialed.

Expecting an answering machine as usual, he was stunned when he heard Gus's voice. "Gus, it's you, oh hi! It's Buddy."

He placed his free hand out of sight under the desk and crossed his fingers.

"Hi, ah...you know Gus, things are just not going too good." He was nervous and his voice sounded funny to him. "In fact," he said trying to keep it light. "Ha, ha...everything's really going to hell. We're not getting much done at all."

There was no response from Gus, only breathing. Buddy looked at Dee and shrugged his shoulders.

Frowning, she whispered, "Go ahead, tell him," she urged.

"Gus," he began again, "I don't know why you want to do all this stuff by yourself. That's what the committee's for."

Silence, from Gus.

"You know Pal, I wasn't supposed to give out that list without making a copy," he said accusingly. He avoided Dee's eye's feeling them bore into the side of his face. Changing his tone, he said, "Somehow, I goofed, I forgot. You know how that is... don't you pal?"

He waited, feeling the sweat under his toupee, running down his back and under his arms. All he could think of was, come on, you son of a bitch, I know you're there, I can hear you wheeze. "Gus!" he shrieked into the phone.

Dee pulled on his arm mouthing, "What's happening?"

Pulling his arm away and putting his hand over the mouthpiece, he whispered back angrily, "I don't know, the bastard hasn't said a word."

"Okay Gus, I know you're having a good time," he said shrilly. "Do you have to keep being a son of a bitch? Let me tell you something...nobody want's you on the committee, got that!"

Breathing hard, Buddy moved this way and that, thwarting Dee's attempts to grab the phone from him. "You listening, you bastard? Nobody wants you!" he screamed into the phone. "And you know it too, don't you?" Buddy's eyes were wild as he gasped for breath, trying to avoid Dee's grabbing hands.

"You're making it worse, for God's sake!" she screeched, but backed down when Buddy suddenly held up his hand, listening.

"Gee Buddy. Sorry you feel that way fella." Gus's voice was oily smooth. "I want you and that dumb blonde wife of yours to understand something."

Desperately wanting to hang up, Buddy was trapped by his own need to know what Gus was up to.

Trying to hear, Dee motioned for Buddy to share the phone but he ignored her, intent only on what Gus was saying.

"As you said, I," he stressed, "have the only 9525ing list, and I have the 9525ing announcements, too, that I am just about to stuff into those 9525ing envelopes."

Buddy took the phone away from his ear momentarily, a puzzled look on his face. What's with the numbers, he wondered. Listening again he heard, "They are going to go out to all the 9525ing classmates, and then they are going to respond."

Dee, trying desperately to hear, kept pulling at Buddy's arm, hearing only bits and pieces of the conversation and it was infuriating her.

"And," Gus was droning on, "it will come back to you, you're address. You'd better make 9525ing sure," said Gus, his voice low and menacing, "that the committee stays together, because now pal...I'm really in charge. Got that?"

Buddy went numb as he listened to the ranting of this madman. His shoulders drooped. One foot slipped off the foot ring, pitching him forward. His free hand grabbed for the desk while his other hung on to the phone for dear life.

"What? What?" Dee kept asking. He tried to ignore her, until she pulled the phone towards her with a quick yank, getting him even more off balance.

Dee did manage to hear the last part and was outraged. "What do you mean, you're in charge? Over my dead body!" she screamed into the phone, wrestling with Buddy, trying to pull the phone out of her grasp. "You can't do that you asshole!" she got off, before Buddy wrenched the phone away from her.

But Dee had such a tight grip on it, he fell backward in his chair clutching the phone to his chest, while Gus ranted, "Get that cunt off the phone!"

Buddy's eyes darted to Dee, praying she didn't hear that, and was relieved to see that she was picking herself up off the floor. Not asking if she were hurt, he figured every man for himself.

He was panting hard as he asked, "Gus...I don't understand you...and I don't think you understand...the situation...nobody is going..to stay on that committee... if you head it."

Buddy listened to the silence that followed.

Then, in his same menacing tone Gus said, "Well Buddy, it's all up to you. We want to have a nice party," he paused, "don't we? What are you going to do, get a new committee together?" Buddy's eyes opened wide looking around the room. My God, he's got us bugged, he imagined, as Gus went on. "As I said before, I'll sure as hell burn this list up. You just think, 50 years of gathering and honing this thing," said Gus caressing the list as he spoke. "And Buddy Boy, I'll burn everything, the list, the announcements and envelopes."

"No, No, don't do that!" Buddy yelled into the phone.

Dee had been glaring at her husband, but now became alarmed. "What?" she asked again for the zillionth time. Buddy held up his hand for silence again, listening. His look convinced her not to interfere, although it galled her.

"Well now, I'm gonna set the wheels in motion and get everything out, and we can go on with our fee-ucking reunion." Gus paused. "What's it gonna be, pal?"

Sweat was pouring down Buddy's face. His toupee, slightly off kilter, was glistening with dampness. He licked his lips. How did everything get so fouled up, he wondered. This was not what was supposed to happen. He and Dee wanted to do such a good job and have the greatest reunion ever. Have everyone love them for it. He even pictured being swept up on his classmate's shoulders, being carried around while the crowd applauded his efforts, forgetting for the moment how old they all were.

Suddenly he felt old. He rubbed his forehead feeling lightheaded. "Gotta go!" he blurted out before he slammed down the phone.

Dee was right on him. "What, what did he say?" she nagged.

Buddy looked at her a long moment, tired beyond belief. "He says he's gonna burn the list and everything else if we don't co-operate."

"Like hell he will," she scoffed.

"He said he would send everything out if we all agreed he will be in charge," he said wearily.

"What else?"

"Uh, he kept using some numbers a lot. Didn't make any sense." He shook his head. "He's nuts." He noticed Dee gave him a strange look. "I'm telling you, if he burns that list and all the other stuff," he looked at her, "we have nothing."

"What number?" Dee asked, ignoring his last remark.

"What?...oh, I don't know. Twenty-five or twenty-nine, something like that. I couldn't keep up with his ravings half the time."

"How did he use it?" she persisted.

"What do you mean? For God's sake Dee!" He saw her frown deepen. Why couldn't she just drop it for once, forget the whole damn thing.

"Buddy!" she said stamping her size four.

"Uh, God," he said tiredly. "Let's see...he tried to remember. "Uh, like the number and envelopes and the number and list, and like that, I think," he said shrugging his weary shoulders.

She was thinking, her eyes blazing as she stared at him. "Wait a minute. Wait a minute...was it five nine or nine five something?" she asked, an intense look on her face.

"Could be, that son of a bitch is crazy."

"Think!" she demanded. "Think Buddy, this is important!"

His eyes glazed over. The last thing he wanted to do was think. His brain felt bruised.

Not Dee. She rarely forgot anything. "Remember this afternoon, how he kept saying a number?" she asked, taking little mincy steps back and forth in the small room.

"Yeah, I think so," he said hesitantly, even though he wasn't sure what he remembered. This afternoon seemed like a year ago, so much had happened. Besides, who could understand any of that mumbling Gus did.

"Well, don't you see?" she asked excitedly. Dee knew she was on to something and could hardly contain herself. She wanted Buddy to confirm her suspicions, which were growing by the minute.

"He's using that number five nine or nine five something instead of some word." She grabbed Buddy's arm in her excitement. "And I think I know what it is!" she exclaimed. "It's that awful word he always uses. You know, the one we all try to ignore?" Buddy nodded, but still looked perplexed.

"Don't you see?" She was willing him to understand and also to see how brilliant she was. "He should be in an institution, not walking around talking in codes."

"But why would he do that?" Buddy asked, not sure of anything at the moment.

"Who knows?" she said smugly.

"Well, if that's true, you'd better not say anything." She gave him a quick smile.   "You know," said Buddy, "until we're sure...you know?"

"We'll see." She gave him a look he knew so well. The I can't promise you anything look. "We'll see," she repeated.

Dee was sure she had it all figured out, and now wanted to move on with new plans. She headed for the door, saying over her shoulder, "There are ways you know, to get rid of people like him," she stated matter of factly as she strode out of the room.

He stared at the empty doorway after she left. "Uh, oh, what does that mean?" he muttered, grateful that the desk was so large, because the walls were starting to close in.

* * * *

Gus whistled, putting down the phone. This had been quite a day, even though he was still trying to put it together. Buddy just put the capper on it for him, telling him he had the only copy of the list. Bonus! Big Bonus!

He relished keeping Buddy off balance, especially Buddy, since it was so easy to do. And that wife of his, he frowned at the thought of her. He shook his large head back and forth. "I just might have to get tough with her."

It did kind of surprise him, he had to admit, when Buddy hung up on him. "9525!" he said. "What's he gonna do? I got him by the balls!" he laughed, then added, "her's too!"

Sitting behind his desk, he couldn't help but admire the envelopes in front of him. Each a work of art, a masterpiece. His eyes fell on the list in its plastic folder. He decided to get some copies made of it, just in case, already worrying that he had the only one. He glanced quickly over his shoulder, as if someone were watching him.

The announcements, stacked neatly, made him smile. There was a reason for them in his plans. "Thanks for printing them, Jake," he said as if Jake were in the room with him. He must remember to mention it when the committee, his committee, got together again.

The list, the envelopes, the announcements. He had it all. His plan was ready. His eyes glistened with pleasure as he picked up an envelope and studied it.

C;5 1Q 6- 72 61 59
9525
Jean Newworth, 0.4.6.

1120 Wilson Avenue

Sonora, 95 37 0

California

112263

Underlined, with different numbers for different thoughts. That's what excited him the most, since he was the only one who knew what those numbers meant.

At one time it was important that somebody understand them, but not now.

Best of all, Buddy and Dee's return address was in the top left corner, with 6.4.9.1. 05 under it, but only on the envelopes for the committee members. He didn't think that would be too difficult, even for those 9525ing fools to understand.

He looked at the phone, willing it to ring. He wanted to continue the conversation. Wanted to keep Buddy squirming. He hated the little toad.

It wasn't just Buddy, he hated everyone. Payback time was near. As always thoughts started to crowd his brain. The Kennedy assassination and how he was treated at school, co-mingling in his mind, all the insults and snide remarks blown way out of proportion becoming bigger than life.

The quarterback had pointed him in the wrong direction. It was his fault, making his family suffer...he still had a copy of the letter to the FBI about the quarterback, naming him as Kennedy's killer. They were blaming the wrong man he told them. Oswald was the wrong man, couldn't they see it?

After all these years he could no longer distinguish truth from fiction, the two events were forever intertwined, making it into a national incident to him. And someone had to pay.

He shook his head, rubbed it back and forth, a far away look in his dark brooding eyes. "9525 it!" he called out, his eyes focusing inward on his plan, going over it again.

Time was on his side and he could do with it whatever he wanted. And he wanted to wait, to savor.

* * * *

Mildred wondered why she hadn't heard from Dee. Usually she was on the phone, checking up on something or other. It seemed strange that she didn't call. It had been almost two weeks. Some of the details of the last meeting were still a little vague, but she did remember that Dee was very quiet just before they left the meeting.

Why do we keep calling them meetings, she wondered. She had to admit, very little got accomplished. Other than her and Jake getting the announcements out, not too much has been done.

Mildred had finally gotten a good night sleep and felt more like her old self after a couple of days. When she told Ma about Gus acting so strange, the sleeping and all, Ma told her a story about a woman she knew years ago.

It seems the woman would go into a deep trance whenever she was in the same room with flickering candles. She had to stop going to church for one thing, and would fall asleep at the dinner table whenever candles were used.

Mildred listened intently, nodding her head. "What happened to the woman, Ma?" she asked when Bella said no more.

"What you mean?"

"Well goodness, candles must have been used a lot in those days, weren't they?" Mildred asked. "What did the poor woman do? What happened to her?"

"She married fat butcher."

"What do you mean she married fat butcher? What does that have to do with candles?"

"Nothing," Bella said innocently.

Mildred looked at her in disbelief. "Honestly Ma!" She wondered sometimes why she bothered, but was soon laughing with Ma joining in.

She went back to work on the reunion program she had laid aside while Bella told her story. She glanced at her mother and smiled. Dear Ma, she always made her feel good.

Mildred found some lovely sayings that could be printed on different pages of the program. She decided to use eight pages in all. A picture of Spinning High on the second page, the evening's program on the following page.

Several pages should be left blank she thought, for notes or phone numbers, addresses or whatever. She had come across a sketch of a beautiful Cypress tree with spreading branches, and knew it would be perfect for the names of the departed classmates printed over it.

Yes, she decided. She liked that idea, but of course she would have to check with Jake and the committee, and made another note to herself. The notes were piling up.

* * * *

For some reason, Janet felt strangely free and smiled as she chopped and stirred. Creating something new in her kitchen always gave her a rush, but this was special.

She still tried to please the Godman, if only through his stomach. Granted, he no longer complimented her outright, but did tell her, "You may fix that again," if he liked it.

Her mind kept returning to the meeting, or lack of it. These were so interesting. She couldn't get over her good luck being on this committee. All the others, for the church, were so...boring.

She went over every minute of it again. She was still shocked about using those swear words on Dee, but relished the part about Gus. Her face felt hot when she thought about him. It's too bad he didn't see me in the pool, she thought, then wondered how she could be thinking such thoughts. Her face burned.

Trying to concentrate on the job at hand, she continued to chop. She kept a special jar in the refrigerator, way, way back, behind other jars. Not that Andy would look in the jar, but just in case, she labeled it, "Poppy Seed Mix."

Opening the jar, she scooped out a full teaspoon to add to the deviled egg and black olive mixture. She smiled as she recalled Andy's comment the first time she fixed it for him.

"Hmmm, crunchy. Not bad!"

She had scooped up the ants from a place in her organic garden that was never sprayed. The jar was almost full as she quickly screwed the top on and put them on a shelf in her potting shed inside a large clay pot, then left them there unattended, for several weeks.

The rest of the yard and shrubs were sprayed quarterly. Andrew could not abide ants or spiders or any crawly thing. She would have to drop whatever she was doing and get rid of any poor creature, if it happened to cross Andrew's path.

She did go to the library to research ants, and if they were edible. She read they had protein or something, so maybe she was doing him a favor. After all, she didn't want to kill him, she only wanted to... what?

She thought about it a lot. Maybe, she just wanted to get even.

* * * *

BEFORE:

Buddy and Dee waited outside the small restaurant, anxiously watching cars drive into the parking lot. He had gone to a great deal of trouble trying to convince the members of the committee to meet with he and Dee. He even had to plead with a few just to come hear him out. When he mentioned Gus would not be there, the problem seemed to vanish. However, it did seem to become some kind of a problem with Janet. In what sounded like real disappointment, she had asked, "Why?"

Buddy dismissed it though, deciding it was just his imagination. Besides, he didn't have time to worry about everyone's state of mind. He just had to get them to the restaurant.

Even convincing Dee to work with the committee had been a hard task. He made her understand, Gus was not just crazy, but crazy like a fox. If Gus burned everything, especially the list, there was nothing they could do. Playing mostly on her vanity, he knew she was already planning what she would wear to the reunion. Of course, he had a few thoughts about his outfit, too.

Dee was not thrilled to be there, even though she let Buddy talk her into it. She only decided to play along simply because she didn't have a firm plan of her own yet. It actually made her sick to her stomach to think that Gus, of all people, would be running things. She and Buddy deserved that power, not that crazy fool.

Shifting his position from one foot to the other, Buddy looked over at Dee. They both hated to wait for anything, and wondered where in the hell they were. He had such a devil of a time getting Leon to join them and didn't expect he'd be too happy today. Even Jake had been obstinate. He hated this!

Mildred was okay, not too reluctant and he smiled remembering her question. Not about Gus, "but would we please stay indoors?"

Dee hated to see all her so-called friends again. She thought she was through with them, that they would be going with a new committee. Damn that Gus. Fat chance now she thought, angry at Buddy for putting her in this position.

She thought about the beautiful gown she was planning to wear, a knockout strapless naturally, with a slit up to her thigh. She smirked, thinking no one else would be able to get away with it, betting none of the gals would have the nerve or the shape.

She felt Buddy tugging at her arm, bringing her out of her reverie. "There's the girls," he said.

"Terrific," she answered sarcastically.

"Come on now hon, you promised." He hugged her. "I want to see my perky little sweetheart," he whispered in her ear.

Melting a tiny bit, she thought, oh well, I only have to see these people a few more times, but that's all!

Disengaging his arm from around Dee and walking towards the women he gave them a hearty, "Hi Ladies, so glad you could make it."

Dee did not move forward with Buddy to greet them, but stood her ground, deciding not to make it too easy for him. Maxie, Mildred and Janet noticed Dee's icy stare and tried to understand what was going on.

Maxie was the first to respond. "Hi you two, how are you?" she asked looking directly at Dee.

"Fine," Dee said a little too quickly.

Maxie and Mildred exchanged glances. Janet walked over to Dee and tried to give her a hug, but Dee did not respond and stood stiffly with her arms at her side.

"Oh hell," muttered Buddy to himself not missing her attitude, but smiling said, "Honey, isn't it just great to see the girls?" Trying to cover up her rudeness he repeated, "So glad you could make it," as she blatantly ignored him.

So flustered by Dee's behavior, Buddy could have gladly kicked her in the ass.

What is her problem? Couldn't she just once help him out instead of acting like such a spoiled brat? Trying to make the best of a bad situation, walked ahead of them and pushed the door open, suggesting, "Let's go in and get a table."

"Of course," smiled Mildred. That poor man, she thought.

Quietly filing in, they seated themselves by a window at Buddy's request. There, they could watch for Leon and Jake, and all turned to stare out the window in the silence that followed. It lasted only a few moments, but seemed like hours to Buddy who hated dissension of any kind.

Finally Maxie spotted Jake and Leon walking towards the restaurant. "Oh, there they are," she said pointing out the window. Dee thought Max seemed a little too excited about a simple thing like that and gave her a suspicious glance.

One could almost hear the sigh of relief from Buddy. Thank God, at least now we can listen to Leon's complaints. That should at least break the ice, he hoped.

"Hello everyone," said Jake. He bent down and kissed Maxie on the cheek. She in turn smiled up at him.

"What's this?" said Dee. "What's going on?"

"Oh, Didn't you know?" Mildred said turning to Dee. "Maxie and Jake have been going out. Isn't that just great?"

Stunned, Dee asked, "You mean like dates?"

"Yes," Jake and Maxie answered smiling.

Dee wanted to hit her. How come she didn't tell her, her very best friend about this, herself? She was furious but took a deep breath to calm herself. "Why that's just wonderful," she cooed. "Maxie and Jake. Well, you make a wonderful looking couple." She started to add, "But don't you think you're both a little too..."

"Happy!" Buddy interrupted loudly, knowing where she was heading, as did the rest.

He felt Dee's glare but refused to look at her. "I agree with Dee, you make a wonderful looking couple." The rest joined in, agreeing with Buddy.

"Thanks you two." Jake was looking at Dee. "Maxie and I are really enjoying ourselves and I guess if it hadn't been for the two of you, insisting we join the committee, we would never have met. So thank you." He leaned down to kiss Dee on her cheek, but she turned her head just in time to have it land on her lips.

Jake realized at once, seeing the glint in her eyes, that she had done it on purpose. He looked down, embarrassed.

Not Dee, she glanced smugly at Maxie to make sure she saw the whole thing and was gratified Maxie didn't miss her meaning. Neither did anyone else.

Buddy squirmed in his seat.

Poor Buddy thought Leon. Poor smuck. "You know Buddy," he spoke up, "I told you I ended up in the hospital after the last meeting "

"Leon?" Maxie and Janet each said, then Janet continued, "What happened, you didn't seem that bad when you left. Of course we were all a little soggy to be sure."

He had their attention now. Leon felt a touch on his shoulder before Jake went to sit down next to Maxie.

"Well, after I left there I was pretty woozy, and then I ran into the back of a car, or it was really a truck I guess." He looked from one to another, gratified to see that they were all concerned."I was okay, just got a bump on my head from the steering wheel, and of course all that water from the pool." He looked accusingly at Dee, who ignored him.

"We're so glad you're okay Leon. That was quiet a day." Jake leaned over and gave his arm a firm grasp. "But I still think it was Gus's urinating in the pool that caused... "

"What?" shrieked Leon. He had forgotten. "Gus peed in the pool! My God, I drank that shit!"

Heads turned in their direction. Now Leon had everyone's attention.

"Calm down Leon, please," said an embarrassed Buddy.

"Calm down. Easy for you, you didn't drink that shit!"

"How do you know? I jumped in and helped get you out the first time for heaven's sake," said Buddy, exasperated.

It was all news to Leon. "What do you mean the first time?"

"It's just that when you were coughing, you were too close to the edge of the pool and rolled in, said Jake. "But," he added quickly, seeing Leon's wild look. "We got you out real quick. Don't you remember?"

"How could I. I was drowning for God's sake!"

118

Dee had had enough. "For heaven's sake Leon, what are you complaining about," she demanded. "You said you were okay, so why aren't you thankful?"

All eyes turned to stare at her.

Knowing she had just gone too far, especially when she saw the look of disgust on Buddy's face, she said contritely, "Well you know what I mean."

"What's wrong with us?" said Maxie, leaning forward in her chair. "Can't we get together without arguing? Gus isn't even here, so we can't blame it on him this time. What's happened to us?" She looked around the table. "We used to be friends." She felt Jake's arm go around her shoulders reassuringly and she leaned back, relaxing.

Surprised by her outburst at first and then stunned into submission, they seemed to get their voices back all at one time.

Quieting them down, Buddy said, "She's right you know. We've been going at each other for each little thing. I'm sorry guys, this is not going like I hoped." He sat quietly collecting his thoughts.

"You know, this was supposed to be a lot of fun," he said wistfully. The other reunion's Dee and I worked on, we really had a great time."

"We really did," added Dee, nodding as she talked, sounding more like her old self.

Buddy appreciated it, and gave her a smile. "You know, I really believe its Gus..."

"Yes," they heartily agreed.

"Wait, hear me out," he said as everyone started to talk to one another. "You know he's been a thorn in my side ever since the first meeting." He noticed the nods. "There is nothing I would like better than to get rid of that guy." Again they nodded and he knew this was not going to be easy.

"I talked to him the other day as you know, and that's why we're here." He looked around the table at their expectant faces. "He's got the list. It's the only copy there is."

They looked at him blankly, until Mildred asked, "Why weren't there copies of that list?"

"I was supposed to make one, but somehow I forgot," Buddy said quietly, "and remember when he provoked me into giving it to him, so he could do the envelopes?"

Those that were leaning forward waiting for his response, sighed and relaxed against the back of their chairs. They were beginning to get the message, and what was there to say?

"Also, he threatened to burn the list if we don't all stay with this committee."

Jake turned to Maxie. "Didn't I tell you he was a devious bastard?"

"Here's something else you're not going to like," said Buddy inwardly flinching. "He says he want's to be in charge, to head the committee."

"Bull shit!" bellowed Leon, outraged. "He can't do that!"

Listening to the exchange with great interest, Janet had to admire the gall of the man. She had no idea what Gus wanted or why he was doing all these things, but she did know she would be very interested in the next meeting, and she hoped there would be one, because she didn't intend to miss it.

"What did he say exactly, Buddy?" Janet wanted to know.

"Besides burning the list? Well, he said he was going to send everything out and put our names on the announcements."

"What's wrong with that?" Jake wanted to know. "We have nothing to hide."

"That wasn't the problem. It's the way he said it...like a threat. You had to have heard it." Buddy looked at Jake. "He's going to do something else, I'm sure of it."

"What? What do you think he'll do?" Maxie asked.

"I'm kind of afraid to find out. You've seen him," Buddy said looking around. "He's disrupted all of our meetings. Caused us to be at each other's throats." He paused. "He's the problem and the solution, I'm sorry to say."

He knew he wasn't doing a good job of talking them into staying on the committee, but he had to be honest with them. Mildred held up her hand. "I have a question." "Sure, Millie, what?" Buddy asked.

"You mentioned a name I believe, at the last meeting."

"Merlin August?" asked Jake.

"I think that was it. I don't remember him, and I believe none of the women here do either. Am I correct?" she asked looking at each of the women, accepting their nods before she continued. "Apparently you men do know something about him." Mildred looked at Jake and the other two. "Why don't you tell us whatever you remember."

Janet perked up. "Great idea Millie!"

But Leon seemed to have lost interest and only said, "I didn't know him that well. Didn't he play football or something?"

"Yes, you're right Leon." Jake leaned forward, putting his elbows on the table. "I believe he was a half-back, but not on the varsity team. We know he was on the swim team. Leon stiffened. He didn't even want to think about water.

"He wasn't anybody that stood out, as I recall," said Jake, "but there was something... gosh it's been so long, so many things get jumbled in my mind now." Gently, Maxie touched his arm.

Suddenly remembering something, Jake started to laugh. "What's so funny?" Janet blurted out. She had been hanging on every word and hoped for a change it was something nice about Gus.

Jake looked at Janet, noting her eagerness. "I think he was the one that ran the wrong way for a touchdown." Jake was still chuckling as he leaned back.

"But what happened?" Janet persisted.

"Nothing," Jake said surprised at Janet's interest and felt compelled to say more, "Ah, I'm sure he was kidded and stuff, but it was a mistake. And there was an article or two in the paper, if I remember."

"I remember that too," Buddy said. "But wasn't he hit in the head before that?"

"I think you're right. I'd forgotten that. That's probably why he went the wrong way," Jake said to Buddy.

"And he's been going that way ever since, I'll bet," Leon said with a laugh. Everyone joined in, but he noticed a nasty look from Janet before she quickly looked down at the table. What's with her, he wondered.

"Was that important?" asked Mildred. She noticed the blank looks she was getting, and added. "I mean was that important as far as the game was concerned." She made it a point to know absolutely nothing about football, thinking it was a rather silly game.

Jake had to smile. "I'd have to say yes. Running the wrong way towards the wrong end zone can be pretty bad, especially if the score is tied, but I can't remember if it was or not."

Mildred gave him a long look. "Would it be important enough for him to...maybe hold a grudge?"

"How could it? It was so long ago. No, no..." Buddy said, dismissing it.

There was silence as the waitress finally approached their table, handing out menus. They had been there about twenty minutes and no one seemed to have given lunch a thought.

Absently studying the menus, Mildred's suggestion nevertheless nagged at a couple of them.

Giving the waitress their orders, they settled back, turning to Leon as he said, "You know, there could be something to what Mildred said. But it seems to me, he's doing these things to us, like he hates us. Now... did one of us do something to him?"

They all looked at Buddy. "Hey, what's with the looks? I didn't do anything to the son of a bitch... he's doing it to me!" he exclaimed.

"Yeah and you're right and he's right, were answered back to him.

"I think we've covered everything we know about Gus, Millie," Buddy said, but hoped and prayed that Dee didn't bring up that stuff about numbers and codes. That would really stir the pot, he thought.

His prayers, were answered, Dee kept silent.

"So," he wanted to get on with his mission. "I think, if we want to have a 50th reunion, and it would be a real shame not to have one..." He sighed, hating to say what he had to. "We just might have to go along with him."

122

"No way!" exclaimed Leon, starting to get up.

"There will be no reunion, I'm telling you Leon. He'll burn the list and even the programs," he pleaded. "There's no way we can get all those addresses together."

"How do you know there isn't another list somewhere?" Leon asked, hating to concede, settling back in his chair.

"I called Spinning High, for God's sake's!" Buddy was getting anxious. "They said there was nothing they could do for us. They mentioned the yearbook, but that doesn't give us the addresses, Leon."

"Well, I don't know, there must be another way," Leon grumbled.

Reaching for anything, Buddy said, "Another thing, we've put a deposit on the ballroom, remember?" He could feel the sweat pouring down his back and under his arms. Why, he wondered, why the hell was he doing this.

But he couldn't stop. "Thirty days have gone by and then some...you see, and we can't get it back, it's forfeited."

"Surely they will understand, if we tell them the circumstances. Don't you think?" asked Mildred.

Buddy looked at her. "You were there Mil, she told us, if we changed our minds, we lost the deposit. After thirty days, that's it!" He hoped he sounded forceful and not shrill.

Seeing the resigned looks on their faces, Dee began to feel sorry for her husband and decided she would try to help him.

"You must know how I feel about that awful man, I was very much against anything that Gus wanted at first, and still am, you can ask Buddy."

They looked at Buddy nodding his head as she talked. "Yeah," he grinned, "I had to do some heavy persuading." He hoped this was going where he wanted it to.

Leon wasn't too impressed with any statement Dee had to make, thinking yeah, I'll bet she had him crawling on his belly, the poor bastard.

"Anyway," continued Dee, "no matter how I feel about him, I think we owe it to our classmates to get this thing finished.

They're depending on us and we did use their money so to speak."

Maxie hadn't been at the hotel luncheon and was a little in the dark since they never got a chance to cover this subject at their so-called meeting. "How?" she asked.

"As you know Maxie, we had a little over $700.00 when we took over from the last reunion committee. We put 500 of that down on the room. So," Dee said as if she had just solved a puzzle for all of them. "That money belongs to the classmates." She dimpled at Maxie. "See?"

"Of course. We'll be responsible for losing it, in other words."

"Right!" Buddy and Dee said together. They looked at each other, smiling. It was the first time in a long time they were thinking alike. Something they often did in the past.

"So, what do you think?" Buddy looked around. "You want to give it one more chance?

Let's see what he has up his sleeve." Then added hopefully, "Maybe we can still save it."

There were some heavy sighs while they thought about it.

"I'm in," said Janet. She couldn't wait.

"So am I," said Mildred. "But I want you to know, I detest that man. And that's for the record."

"Who doesn't?" Buddy agreed, "and so noted,"

Jake and Maxie were looking at each other. "What do you think?" he asked her. Then, not waiting for her to answer, he added, "I'll go with whatever Maxie says."

Maxie wasn't sure she liked being put on the spot like that. "Well, I ah, you know you're a rat Jake," she said looking at him fondly.

"I know," he smiled at her. They leaned towards each other for a moment, lingering as their foreheads touched.

"Aww!" grinned Mildred, unable to suppress her fondness for the two of them. "Isn't that the sweetest thing?" she said, turning to Janet sitting next to her.

Janet was smiling blissfully, getting her own thrills with her private water balloon. Naturally Mildred assumed she was agreeing with her, and looked back at Jake and Maxie.

Consumed by the green-eyed monster, Dee looked away.

"Okay," said Maxie getting over the embarrassment of Mildred's words. "What the heck, in for a penny, in for a pound, besides…I'm curious. I want to see what he's up to, too," she grinned.

Buddy breathed a sigh of relief. So far so good, six out seven, not bad he told himself. But now... Leon. He crossed his fingers under the table for good luck. "What about you Leon?"

Leon hated Gus and knew it would be intolerable to be in the same room with him again. He looked around at these people, not friends really, except Buddy. But how much was he supposed to give for this reunion he wondered.

It had become perilous for him especially. He couldn't forget or forgive the fact he almost drowned or was humiliated by Dee, whom he disliked intensely. Besides, he'd already told Martha he was going to tell them he was sure as hell through, no matter what. He was trying to hold on to that decision, but like Maxie, he was curious, too. "Dammit, I guess I'm in."

"Oh," said Buddy, actually surprised. He had expected the worst, knowing how stubborn Leon could be, and had filled his lungs with air preparing for the big discussion as his breath came out in a rush. Arguments he planned to use had nowhere to go and seeped out of him along with the air from his lungs, leaving him deflated.

After a long pause, he pulled himself together. "Well, thank you Leon. I really do appreciate it. I really do." He knew he was gushing when he felt Dee's unapproving eyes on him.

"Excuse me Buddy," said Janet, when do you think the next meeting will be?" She was ready.

Buddy hadn't thought that far ahead. His efforts were all focused on getting them to come to this meeting, so now he was at a loss.

"What do you think?" he asked the group. "We're almost into September, so... what? Want to take a month off, maybe go for late October."

"What about Gus?" Maxie asked.

"Screw Gus!" replied Buddy. A few laughs followed. "I'll let him know." He puffed up, feeling he still had a little control.

Some of them had plans of their own and were happy for the respite. Not Janet, however, disappointment showing on her face.

Noticing, Mildred asked, "What's the matter, Janet? Don't you want to get away from this for awhile?"

"Oh, sure," Janet lied. "But...I'll miss you all," was all she could think of.

Those that overheard were touched by Janet's remark, but Dee surprised them all. She burst into tears.

"I'm sorry everyone," she wailed, her voice rising. She was oblivious to the fact the waitress had just brought their sandwiches and that other patrons were again turning to stare at them, making Buddy's stomach do nervous flip flops. "I've been a real stinker," she sobbed. "Will you all forgive me?"

Stunned at first by her outburst, they finally responded as quietly as possible while exchanging plates with each other. The poor waitress, thinking maybe she had done something wrong, just laid the plates down anywhere and quickly moved away. "Will you?" she asked again, dabbing at her eyes.

"Yes, sure, of course, um hum," they answered not knowing what else to say or do. Leon, on the other hand, barely nodded. He wanted to clap his hands together. What a performance, he thought.

* * * *

"I think we convinced them all, don't you?" Buddy said as he drove through the traffic with Dee at his side.

She had been very quiet after her outburst at the restaurant and now sat stonily staring out the window. She wondered if maybe she had overdone it a bit.

She was somewhat sorry, but she had to make them think she was really sorry. After all, if they were going to have to still work together, she needed reassurance that her friends still loved her.

What really galled her, was Maxie and Jake. Damn her, she thought, she made me look like a fool again. Why didn't she tell me after all, aren't we supposed to be best friends? The least she could have done was say something to me first. She fidgeted in her seat. Mildred and Janet knew all about it... ahead of me, for God's sake.

"Dee?"

Buddy's voice startled her. "What?" she gave him a quick look.

"I said, I think we got them all to stay with it, don't you think? I know they all said they would stay, but you never can tell." He gave her a sideways glance. What's with her anyway, crying like that in the restaurant, he wondered.

She nodded her head, and turned back to stare out the window. He had a suspicion she really wasn't as upset as she wanted them to think she was.

"Dee?" He felt like giving her a bad time, relishing the moment.

She turned to him again. "I said yes, I nodded my head didn't I? That means yes," she said somewhat surly, but seeing his expression, toned it down a bit. "I noticed Leon was kinda hard to convince." She gave him a long look before turning back to the window. "I could live a thousand years without seeing him again. I almost wish he had said no," then added, "He's a real pain in the ass."

Buddy had to smile. Look who's calling who a pain in the ass, Leon's probably calling her the same thing right this minute and she knows it. "Leon, oh I'm really glad he decided to stay on the committee," he said innocently, his smile getting broader. He glanced over to see her reaction and got a kick that she was squirming in her seat. He couldn't help it, he had to chuckle.

Dee ignored him, knowing he was trying to get her goat. They rode in silence until Buddy said, "I guess I'll have to call

Gus, or Merlin, whatever, and tell him we'll have the next meeting in late October."

Dee stared out the window.

* * * *

"Why on earth did you leave it all up to me?" asked Maxie, sitting in her favorite chair. She had just gotten home after dropping the ladies off and the first thing she did was pick up the phone. "I wanted to leave it all up to you, and you beat me to it. "She laughed. "We really do think a lot alike, don't we?"

Jake was enjoying listening to her voice, the sound of intimacy in it. He smiled, "Yes, I noticed that too."

"What?" she asked, anxious for the answer.

"That we think alike, and I'm sorry I didn't let you go first, I hope you didn't mind too much, did you?" He was looking out the window at the garden, noticing it looked a bit seedy.

"No, not really, but I thought, you know, when we talked about it the other night."

"Mmmmm, mm," he agreed, still staring at Fran's garden.

"We weren't going to be involved with that committee and I thought, you know?" She was losing her train of thought at this point, thinking about the other night...with Jake. It was a lovely night.

"Right, I do know." But Jake was thinking about what Buddy said, "You know, about the list being burned..." Maybe the garden needed more water, he thought. "You know Maxie, it would be such a pity, like Buddy said, if we didn't have the 50th reunion, wouldn't it?" He realized he no longer dwelled on the garden, when he added, "I really want to show us off"

She wasn't expecting that and smiled at the us part. "Oh Jake, what a lovely thing to say."

"It's what I've been thinking about you know...a lot...and I want us to go to that reunion together." Jake said tenderly.

Hearing a catch in his voice, when he added, "I would be so proud," overwhelmed Maxie. She suddenly knew, here was her Boris.

No, she told herself, not Boris. Her Jake. She liked the sound of that, her Jake.

"So would I Jake, so would I," she said softly, close to tears. "We'll just have to make sure, won't we, that Gus doesn't screw it up for us."

* * * *

"I don't know why I let Buddy talk me into it again," Leon complained, sitting on the back yard swing. Moving slightly to and fro, it creaked from his weight. He noticed that the air was filled with perfume from Martha's roses.

She planted them right after they moved into the house, thirty-five years ago. Starting to relax a bit, he lit one of his cigars.

"If you're going to smoke that thing, I'm going into the house," said Martha sitting across from him.

"Oh come on Martha. We're outside for God's sake!" He shook his head. "Look, I'll blow the smoke away from you. See?" he said, turning his head away so that the large gray puff of smoke drifted away from her.

Mesmerized, she watched a bee become engulfed in the deadly smoke, and was sure she saw its tiny body leave a trail of smoke behind it. Probably coughing, she imagined, as it somehow managed to fly away.

"Why did you let them talk you into it?" she asked, taking as few breaths as she dared.

"I'm a Goddamn jerk, that's why. I can't stand Gus, and Dee, Jeez....you should have seen the act she pulled today."

"What do you mean act?"

"She turned on the faucet, real fast. Too fast, if you ask me." In his excitement he puffed, forgetting to turn his head. Martha quickly raised the tissue to her nose.

He got the message. How come she always has a tissue handy, like it's growing out of her Goddamn hand for crying out loud? I could live forever, and never have one when I need it.

In a nasally voice, pinching her nose with the tissue, Martha asked, "What about her?"

"Who?" Anger had replaced his train of thought.

Martha could hardly breathe. "Dee, for heaven's sake," she said accusingly, wanting to get away from that cigar.

"Ah, yeah... like I said, she'd been acting like a real bitch, and then all of a sudden she's crying, asking us all to forgive her. What crap!" Leon took a long drag, and blew it out.

"Did you?" asked Martha waving the Kleenex back and forth against the cloud of smoke.

Leon frowned. Does she have to be so damn obvious, he asked himself. We're outside for Christ's sake!

Everything was really bugging him lately. Maybe it was from almost drowning. He still couldn't remember a few things, like how he hit that truck, and that bugged him. His list of things that bugged him was growing.

It just wasn't any fun, and Buddy promised we'd have a great time, that's what he said. "Like hell!" exploded out of him along with a cloud of smoke completely engulfing Martha.

"That's it!" she said getting up. "See what you did?" She coughed, thinking of that poor bee. She coughed again, "It's just too much for me…and now thanks to you…I got a headache!"

Martha was getting near the top of that list.

* * * *

Two weeks had gone by since the get-together at the restaurant, but Janet had very little time to think about it. The Godman had kept her busy with preparations for the upcoming Church picnic. He had found all kinds of irritating problems with everything she did.

She knew he did not appreciate her being away from her duties to attend the reunion meetings. She was beginning to hate her life. The luncheons, Bible study and meetings for this and that, were getting to be too much. Andrew's demands, complaints and criticisms left her drained.

The reunion committee meetings began to be all she had to look forward to. They were beyond anything she had ever experienced. Exciting, nothing like her boring life with Andrew.

Janet knew she was wishing her life away, but she wished for October. She wondered what Gus was doing, then wondered why she was wondering. The phone rang, interrupting her thoughts.

Wearily, she picked it up. "Hello," she said. Her shoulders slumped as she listened to the irritating voice of one of the women on her food committee, droning on and on.

Finally after what seemed forever, she was able to get a word in. "Gladys!" she said using a stronger tone than she intended. Or was it? "I'm sure you can figure that out for yourself. Just make your usual recipe, it will be fine."

She rolled her eyes, wondering why they always had to bug her, adding "I have to get something out of the oven, so I'll see you at the next meeting, bye." She hung up.

"And screw you, Gladys!" she said to the dead phone.

"What! What did you just say?" demanded Andrew, walking into the kitchen at that precise moment.

Her hand went to her mouth as she slowly turned to face him.

"I'm waiting Janet!" he said, anger making his cheeks flush.

When she removed her hand from her mouth, Andrew became visibly shaken. She had a wide grin on her face. She was not contrite as he expected her to be, rendering him momentarily speechless.

Janet was enjoying herself. No longer did she hold back what she was thinking. "I said screw you Gladys!" Looking at him closely, she asked, "Didn't you ever want to say that to someone Andrew?"

"Of course not!" he said, appalled at the mere mention of such a thing.

"Come on Andy, fess up," she teased, relishing the moment.

"How could you do that?" he said loudly, grabbing her arm. "Did she hear you?" he asked, his face close to hers.

Pulling her arm away, she waited, letting him stew a little longer. "No," she finally said.

"Thank God!" he said throwing up his arms.

"But if I had to listen to much more of that pap, I'm sure she would have," she added. It failed to bother her that his face had turned a beet red, almost purple. "You don't have to worry Andrew, I already hung up." She had hoped there was still some humor left in him, but disappointedly she could see, there was none.

"How... how could you say such a thing," he sputtered. "What's gotten into you? I don't know, I just don't know." He stared at her for a moment, his eyes bulging.

"It's that reunion thing, isn't it? What goes on at those meetings?" He didn't wait for an answer. "That's exactly what it is. You have been thoughtless and non-caring since you started with those people."

Now it was Janet's turn to get indignant. "Those people?" she asked.

"Yes. You're job is to work for our people, the good people of the church," he said self-righteously. "That's all you should concern yourself with." He had moved closer to her, leaning forward with his hands on his rather broad hips.

"Well, Janet, I want you to know you're through with that. You will not go to another meeting. I'm sure they can find other people to do," he paused looking for words, "whatever you do. Do I make myself clear?"

When she didn't answer, he repeated, glaring at her, "Do I make myself clear?"

She glared back at him, anger rising inside her. "Yes, Andrew, yes you do. And you know what?" she paused for effect. "Screw you too!"

* * * *

Mildred was upset as she read the ticket she took from under the windshield wiper. She had only been in the shop for a few minutes. She looked around for some explanation. No red, green or anything on the curb, no signs anywhere.

Bella was sitting in the front seat, just the top of her head and eyes showed. She could hardly see over the bottom of the window Mildred noticed. My gosh, she thought, Ma is going to just disappear below that window one of these days.

"Ma, did the policeman say anything to you?" she asked, opening the car door on the driver's side and sliding in.

"What policeman?"

"The one who wrote this ticket," she said crossly, holding the paper in front of Bella's face.

"I see no policeman."

"How could you not see him?" she asked incredulously. "He must have stood there," she pointed to the right front fender, "and wrote out this ticket, plus putting it under the wiper." She waved it in front of Bella's face again.

"Stop that!" Bella made a feeble attempt to grab at the irritating piece of paper. Waiting for Mildred for at least a half an hour in the hot car was tiring especially since she couldn't figure out how to open the window. All she wanted to do was lay down. "You in there long, long time," she said accusingly.

"I was not." How could it be? "It couldn't have been more than a few minutes... I'm sure," she added slowly, looking at Bella. Bella looked away.

She had gone into the shop to look for the 50-year seals to put on the outside of the programs. Looking through some catalogs couldn't have taken more than a few minutes...could it?

Mildred didn't want to think about that now, she just wanted to know why she had gotten a ticket. There was no meter next to the car, she checked. Stretching her neck, she looked back down the street. No meters.

Then she saw it. A sign was partially hidden by a low hanging branch. She got out of her car to get a better look at it. "No parking, between the hours of 6AM and 12PM," it read.

She looked at her watch. It read 10:03, and it was the morning. She got back in the car and checked the clock on the dashboard. It read 10:07.

"What's wrong with these people," she said. "I parked legally, for heaven's sake. That sign said 6 to 12PM, and it's only 10:03." Her mind at that point could not differentiate the 6AM part, and honed in only on the 12PM part.

She started the car, heading for the nearest police station.

Mildred had no intention of leaving Bella in the car again, so after parking in a lot designated for the police station, she put a complaining Bella into her chair, and pushed her through the automatic doors.

Feeling wronged by the powers that be, but absolutely certain in her mind that she had done nothing wrong, she marched up to the policeman seated behind a large desk, impatiently waiting while he continued to write.

"Young man," she said.

Without looking up, he told her, "Be right with you."

"Millerd, pay the fine."

Mildred leaned down. "Ma, I have to do this. They made a mistake."

"Millerd, I tired."

"I know, Ma, but please give me a minute."

"That's what you say when you went in store."

"And it was!" Mildred's voice was rising, not wanting to get into that again. She had to keep focused on the ticket.

"Bully Sheet!" Ma's reedy little voice rang out.

"Ma!"

That brought the policeman's head up, and then down again quickly. He tried to hide his amusement by coughing and shuffling the papers he was working on. When he looked up again, he could only see the top of Bella's head with single corkscrew wisps of white hair standing straight up like antenna, and her piercing eyes. He avoided the beady gaze, and concentrated on Mildred. "Yes Mam, how can I help you?"

Mildred waved the ticket in front of him. "This. I was given this ticket, illegally." She was waving it back and forth. "I want you to know I have never, ever gotten a ticket!" She continued to wave it nervously, until he managed to grab it away from her.

After studying it for a moment, he said, "You parked illegally."

"I did no such thing!" Her voice became shriller.

"Yes Mam, you did." He stood up. "There was no parking between the hours of 6AM and 12PM." He looked back at the ticket. "The ticket was written at 9:45AM." He sat down again.

"Yes, 6 to 12PM. Now, I was parked there at 9:45" Mildred looked at him as if he were an idiot, waiting for him to see his mistake. When he continued to stare at her, she added, "How can you give me a ticket? I was there before ten o'clock, no where near 6 o'clock," in disbelief at his stupidity.

Bella grabbed Mildred's jacket, and pulled a couple of times. "Millerd, pay the ticket."

"I'm busy Ma!" she said impatiently. "Besides, why should I pay for something I didn't do?"

"Mam?" The policeman said, while looking around for someone to help him out. "Mam?" he repeated. "I don't think you understand... "

"What?" she interrupted. "What do you mean I don't understand? Of course I understand. I was a high school teacher, for heaven's sake!"

"I just meant that those signs can be confusing.... "

He had gone too far. "You think I'm confused?" she interrupted again, wanting to scream.

"Millerd!"

"What?"

"Pay the ticket."

She ignored Bella. The policeman shrugged his shoulders, and waved for another man to come over.

"Jensen?" the man asked, as he approached the desk. "What seems to be the problem?"

"Sir, this woman believes she was given this ticket by mistake." He handed the slip of paper over to the other man, who quickly scanned it and then looked up at Mildred.

"You parked in a time zone. It was 6AM to 12PM. What's the problem?" You were ticketed at 9:45AM." He looked quizzically at Mildred, and then down at Bella. Bella gazed back.

Mildred thought if she heard those numbers one more time she would lose it. "I have been trying to tell you, it wasn't even 6 o'clock yet," Mildred said again, giving them the benign look she used to give her slow students.

"You obviously are confused Lady."

That did it for Mildred, while the seated policeman looked down, unnerved by Bella's steady beady gaze. Even though she was overly sensitive, especially now, with her own doubts and her episodes, Mildred was determined.

Uncertainty did raise its head, but she pushed it away, refusing to acknowledge it. She knew what she read and she knew she was right. She would not back down, she would not be dismissed.

With her feet firmly planted, she glared down at this impertinent young man, and then at his partner.

"Confused! I am not confused. You are the ones confused," she said and demanded, "I am waiting for you to tear up that ticket. I will say it one more time, I was nowhere near there at 6PM." She paused for a moment. "And I certainly know how to read a sign," she added angrily.

The two men looked at each other, a silent agreement passing between them. "Alright Mam," the policeman behind the desk said, tearing the ticket in half. "See, I tore up the ticket. Now please calm down, and we are sorry for you're inconvenience. Alright?"

Somewhat mollified, Mildred looked at the policeman. "Thank you," she said, even thought she felt they were treating her like some kind of addled child.

"I knew you, well not you personally, but someone in the department had made a mistake." Then, with as much dignity as she could muster, she turned to Bella. "We can go now Ma," not adding, "see, I was right!" Though she was thinking it.

Grabbing hold of Bella's wheelchair, she turned her around and pushed her towards the door. As they were going through the automatic doors, she thought she heard laughter from behind. Glancing back, she saw the two men doubled up over the desk.

"Millerd!" said Bella, when Mildred stopped pushing. "Let's go."

Automatically, she started to push Bella out the door, but something began to bother her.

Driving home, she concentrated on the road, glancing occasionally at Bella, noticing she was looking straight ahead at the dashboard since she was too low to see out of any windows. Maybe I should put a pretty picture there, she considered, so Ma would have something interesting to look at.

"Millerd," Bella began quietly.

Mildred looked down at Ma. "What?" she said absently.

"Why you no understand that ticket?"

Mildred groaned. "Not you too." She felt betrayed, her brain numb.

"6 A.M. Millerd. 6 A.M. to 12 P.M."

"Yes, 6 A.M., right. She stopped at a red light. "Between 6 A.M. and 12..." Then as if a bell went off in her head, she realized she had made a terrible mistake. "Oh my God ...what have I done?.. Ma?" She looked down at Bella with wide-open eyes.

Bella started to cackle.

Mildred couldn't believe her ears. "There's nothing funny about this, Ma. My God, I was wrong, so wrong... and I was so sure I was right....honest Ma, I was so sure," she said with wonder. "Those men back there... my God...I went to the police station."

It was ridiculous and she wanted to dwell on her mistake, but Bella's laugh was starting to get to her. "My God, they must have thought I was a raving lunatic." She put her hand to her mouth, suppressing a giggle.

Horns started to honk behind her. Ma was making a strange sound, but Mildred soon realized it was just a louder cackle.

Cars were pulling around them with angry stares and one person even gave her the finger. Now, that was funny she thought, and started to laugh, completely forgetting she was sitting in her car, stopped at a light that had gone from red to green, and back to red again.

Helplessly, she sat there swept up in the laughter, until it verged on the edge of hysteria.

* * * *

THE MEETING: October 7th, 1995

Seated in Buddy and Dee's Patriotic Room, the committee members waited for their new leader. A brisk breeze was coming through the wide-open windows, the new sheer curtains Dee had recently purchased, were dancing, billowing out into the room.

As usual Leon was grumbling. This time because Gus was late, making them wait for him. "Just like that rat to keep us waiting."

Buddy gave him a nervous smile. "Take it easy Leon." He did agree with him, but didn't want him to know it. "He'll be here, don't worry." Under his breath he added, "He's just being his crummy self."

Unhappily, Dee looked around. Here they were in her house again, even though she had vowed the last time that that was it. Now she had to act like nothing happened. She felt her lip twitch, the beginning of a miserable condition when she was stressed.

Damn, now it started and it's all Buddy and Gus's fault she told herself, putting a hand to her mouth. Janet and Mildred had their heads together, Dee noticed. I'll bet their sharing another secret, they don't want me to know about. Some friends. Her eyes drifted to Maxie and Jake.

And just look at those two. She shifted in her red and white striped chair, wanting to punch out the little hard star pillow she was holding in her lap. They're acting like a couple of teenage jerks, if you ask me. Her lip twitched again, the tic's getting closer together.

She could not turn away and forget it, not Dee. Does he have to have his arm around her like that? Jealousy seeped out of her pores. They're a couple of old fools, she was thinking when a sudden gust of wind blew the curtains straight out, almost enveloping the love birds sitting on the small oversized plaid loveseat.

139

Good, she thought, maybe that will act like a bucket of ice water. They sure as hell need something to distract them. She made no move to close the window.

Anxiously watching Dee, Buddy noticed the twitch. He knew it always happened when she was extremely upset and silently prayed she would not make a scene. His prayer was interrupted by the doorbell chiming out, "Oh What A Beautiful Morning," each note loud and clear.

He hoped Dee would answer it, but she didn't move, so he jumped out of his chair and went to the door.

Pushing his way in as if he owned the place, Gus proceeded down the hall, with Buddy following. "There's nothing fancy going on in there is there?" Gus asked over his shoulder.

"What do you mean?" asked Buddy not understanding the question.

Gus stopped to turn and look at him. "No fee-ucking mirrors or flashing lights, you know...like the last time?" Gus wanted to make darn sure he wasn't walking into another trap.

He really is goofy, Buddy thought, then answered lightheartedly, "Oh no, just plain old all of us." When Gus stared at him blankly he had to look down, feeling guilty for some unknown reason.

"Look who's here," Buddy said as they entered the room. At least he should try to get it off to a good start, he thought, but when nobody responded, slinked over to the nearest empty chair and sat down. Fuck the whole thing, he thought.

"Well now," said Gus, "how's my committee?"

Leon squirmed in agitation, muttering under his breath, "You sorry son of a bitch."

Janet, talking to Mildred looked up when Gus came into the room, eagerness flowing out of her. She gave him a big smile. The rest stared glumly, in stony silence.

Maxie knew what Jake meant when he gently squeezed her arm and tried not to laugh. But after checking the other faces in the room, she became a little concerned. It looked like a lynch mob.

Janet's big smile surprised her at first, but then dear Janet is just nice to everyone. It's her nature, she told herself.

Dee's lip twitched like mad, while Mildred stared passively.

Gus did not miss any of it, relishing their discomfort. Leon looked constipated, Buddy just looked stupid with that 9525 rug on his head, and Dee he was happy to see, was twitching away for some 9525ing reason. Forget that schoolteacher, she looked like she had a spring up her ass and the other two, sitting so cozy together, he ignored.

He did do a double take on Janet who was grinning at him. What's with her he wondered, then never gave it another thought.

Feeling like a big man, Gus looked down on Buddy, almost lost in one of the big blue and white chairs. "Good going Buddy, I see you kept everyone together." He rubbed his large shiny dome. "Now that's what I call fee-ucking great!" smiling at Mildred's very obvious shudder.

"I'm not going to blow any smoke up you're asses. I think you all know now that I'm holding all the cards here, since I have this here fee-ucking list." He fanned himself with several sheets of paper, copies of the precious list, flaunting it.

"What the hell do you want Gus?" asked a disgusted Jake, removing his arm from around Maxie's shoulders. He had had enough. He leaned forward, "Or, shall we call you Merlin?"

The subtle change in Gus was hardly noticeable at first. He stared at Jake with hatred, the papers in his hand crunching up as he made a fist.

"Where did you get that name?" he asked menacingly, moving towards Jake, while Maxie tugged on Jake's shoulder, trying to make him lean back, away from Gus.

Slowly Jake stood up. Since buying expensive athletic shoes, and going daily to the gym for workouts, he had almost become a new man, or felt like one anyway. Practically gone was the man he had become after Fran's death. Now he felt stronger, straighter, surer of his step and definitely more of a threat to Gus.

The two of them were standing in the middle of the room with Gus looking up into Jake's face, and what he saw there he didn't like. Jake was too sure of himself.

"I remembered what you did years ago at Spinning," said Jake, a slight smile on his face.

From the safety of his chair, Leon chimed in, "Me too!" but shrunk a little at the look Gus turned on him.

"What is this?" Gus asked, turning back to Jake. "It was that fee-ucking quarterback's fault, not...not mine," he said somewhat defensively, feeling that old pressures begin to build.

Mildred had been drifting a bit, thinking she was back in her classroom, when that awful word entered her subconscious.

Before anyone could react to Gus's weird words, Mildred shot out of her chair and to everyone's surprise, pushed Jake out of the way. Facing a startled Gus, she began berating him. "That will be enough of that language young man. You will have to go to the office immediately. We cannot have you disrupting our class like this."

Startled at first like the rest of the committee, Gus regaining most of his composure, sneered, "Hey! What the fee-uck is she talking about?" He tried to dismiss her with, "Sit down and be quiet, you crazy old broad!"

Red-hot rage grew in Mildred. No one spoke with such disrespect to a teacher. Never! "WHY DO YOU SAY FEE-UCK? THERE IS NO SUCH WORD IN THE DICTIONARY, WHAT YOU MEAN IS F U C K!" she shouted, spelling it out.

"Mildred, dear!" Janet reached out to touch her. "Mildred come on, let's sit down, come on dear." But Mildred would have none of it.

Disentangling herself from Janet's grasp she went at Gus again. Practically jumping up and down in front of him, her sharp nose inches from his, she continued to scold him.

"And F U C K," she spelled out again, "is also not in the dictionary. I hate that word, it is vile, vile, and has no place in decent conversation, nor in mixed company." She had him backed up, pressed against the plaid wallpaper, his face a deep magenta.

"Get her the... "he found he couldn't use his word. She had spoiled it for him. "YOU BETTER GET HER AWAY, OR I'll KNOCK HER ON HER SKINNY ASS," he hollered to anyone, trying to sidestep her. She stayed with him, the two appearing to do a strange synchronized dance, infuriating him even more.

Rushing to Mildred, Maxie and Jake tried to pull her away, amazed at how much strength she had. Janet stepped back, out of the way, stunned by the scene in front of her.

Buddy also rushed up to help, but instead, his wide open eye ran into Mildred's elbow as she yanked it backwards with great force to avoid contact from anyone trying to deter her Like a shot it knocked him down. "Ouch," he wailed writhing on the floor, his hand plastered to his already swelling eye. "Shit, that hurts! Owwwwww!"

Mildred, forgotten for the moment, Jake and Maxie concentrated on the prostrate Buddy.

Thinking Gus had hit her man, Dee flew into the melee. "Pick on somebody you're own size, you pervert!" she yelled up at Gus as she knelt down next to Buddy, trying to pry his hand away from his eye, but he wouldn't let her. "Ow! Ow!" was all he could say.

Out of harm's way, Leon stood next to Janet, trying to decide whether to flee or get a better look could only stare in total surprise. "Jesus!" he muttered.

"Amen!" agreed Janet, moving closer to him after Mildred rebuffed her. She could see things were totally out of hand, but felt a wondrous excitement.

This is what she craved, what she needed. But Mildred's strange behavior worried her, as did Gus's threats. Surely he wouldn't hurt Mildred, but she had to admit, he did look scary.

"SOMEBODY GET HER AWAY FROM ME!" roared Gus. Switching the list to his other hand, and thinking of bopping this nutty school teacher, he raised his other fist in a warning.

Standing up, Dee put herself in Gus's view so he couldn't miss her. "Hey Merlin," she taunted, "why don't you try you're code words, ninety-five or fifty-nine something or other?"

Buddy sat up at that, still holding his eye. "Goddamn it. No Dee no!" he yelled. She promised not to bring that up, he told her Gus wasn't right in the head. Knowing this could be bad, he moaned as his stomach began to burn, matching the intense pain in his eye.

Gus's head snapped towards Dee, a look of surprise, then rage. How did that witch know about that, he wondered. No one is supposed to know my secret numbers. He felt a scathing hatred for her. Mildred was still standing close to him, too close and he was tired of it. "Get the hell away from me!" he said giving her a powerful shove with both fists.

Flying backwards, she took Maxie and Jake with her, stumbling over a still sitting Buddy where they all landed in a heap. Sprawled in every direction, they lay too stunned to move.

Not so Dee, her hands on her hips and her size four's planted firmly into her lime green rug, she faced her enemy.

"What are you gonna do now?" mocked Dee. "You gonna shove me too Merlin?" she taunted, daring him, too angry to be afraid. He had ruined all her plans and she wasn't going to let him get away with it.

Thinking she saw a flash of fear in his glinty eyes, she told herself, I got you now, you shit. But before she could say anything else, he whipped out a Bic lighter from his pocket and began rubbing his thumb furiously against the wheel, producing a long flame.

"I'll show you what I'm gonna do, you witch!" he screamed holding the lighter under the pages of the list and setting them on fire.

Unable to untangle themselves from each other, the group on the floor, all senior citizens, were not as agile as they once were. They knew you just don't get up, first you check for broken bones.

Viewing the situation with his one good eye, Buddy yelled from the floor, "Stop him!"

"Call the police! Call the police!" Dee screeched trying to make a grab for the lighter, but it was way over her head.

Not too interested in the antics of Gus and Dee at the moment, Jake finally managed to pull himself up, then carefully helped each of the ladies up. "You okay?" he asked each of them.

Her dignity more bruised than the rest of her, Maxie complained, "We could have been hurt you know, we're not kids anymore." Noticing Jake rub his shoulder she added, "See, I knew it, you're hurt aren't you?" she asked with concern.

"No not really, just twisted something or other, but I'm fine."

Mildred could not understand what she was doing on the floor, or how she got there. The wind seemed to have been knocked out of her for a moment. She lay there helpless, until she heard Jake and Maxie asking her if she was all right.

"Yes... I think so," she answered vaguely, allowing them to help her up.

The commotion going on between Gus and Dee made them turn. When Dee yelled police, Gus heard instead, FBI, and panicked. They killed Kennedy, was all he could think. He started to run, the burning papers still clutched in his fist as if the demon from hell was after him.

She was.

"Ninety-five, Twenty-five," he was yelling while turning to look over his shoulder and ran into one of the sheer curtains blowing inward.

The curtains, like the rest of the furniture in the room, had not been treated with any kind of flame retardant. Dee had declined, since there was no fireplace in that room, or no smoking allowed, she figured why spend the money.

The curtain quickly ignited with a quiet swoosh, sending little bits of flaming material here and there. Some landed on the large patriotic couch and several of the striped chairs, matching the curtain in their ability to ignite.

Dee usually quick on her size fours stopped her pursuit and could only stand transfixed at the chaos spinning around her. Bits of burning paper and curtain material danced and swirled in the breeze of the open windows.

The other curtains soon picked up sparks and added their contribution.

Buddy, still clutching his eye, somehow managed to get on his feet, ran after Gus. A bit of the burning curtain landed on his head setting his toupee on fire. He looked like a flaming Tiki Torch moving towards Gus.

Noticing the blazing toupee, Jake grabbed a star pillow from a chair and gave Buddy a couple of forceful smacks on his head, causing his weakened knees to buckle.

In the confusion, Gus made a clean getaway, but the pillow became a flaming star, and Jake had to toss it.

"Call the Fire department!" someone screamed as the wind continued to fan the small fires around the room.

The little pillows were the first things picked up to beat out the flames, since they were everywhere and handy. But unfortunately, they were not the answer. Flaming stars under different circumstances, would certainly be unique.

"Did anyone call the Fire department or 911?" was yelled again, and Buddy still a bit stunned, ran towards his den.

The Patriotic Room was becoming quite colorful. Red and blue flames reached out, consuming more and more of the contents in the room. The rug however, did not burn. Wherever burning bits landed on it, it oozed like an open sore.

Leon, Janet and Mildred, who had finally come back to reality, were busy trying to beat out the fires, but Leon quickly saw that it was an impossible task.

The smoke was making it hard to breathe. "This place is a Goddamn jinx!" he gasped. Almost drowning in their damn pool was one thing, but he wasn't about to be burned to a crisp in this crazy damn room.

"We gotta get out!" he screamed, trying to compete with smoke alarms going off in other parts of the house. "Come on, we can't stay here!"

Janet was the closest to him, so he grabbed her arm and pulled. She in turn grabbed for Mildred who was trying desperately to get a hold on Dee. They had to forcibly pull her out of the room.

Dee had become fascinated by the colors of the flames. "Look Buddy, it's even prettier than my mirrored ball," she said. "Buddy, Buddy, look!" she called out as they dragged her, clutching the only surviving star pillow to her chest.

Buddy, Maxie and Jake ran out the sliding glass doors to the patio, and made their way to the front of the house. They huddled with the others as neighbors began to come out of their houses, the flames mirrored in their eyes.

The wail in the distance from the responding fire engines grew louder with each passing moment.

"Did Gus get out?" Janet asked hopefully.

"I hope so," wheezed Buddy, his ratty toupee still smoking. "Cause I'm going to kill that sorry son of a bitch," he said in quiet despair, watching the flames.

The pathetic little group stood outside. Their clothes, hair and skin, streaked with an unusual red and blue hue, watched as the fireman labored to save the rest of Buddy and Dee's dream home.

The meeting from start to finish, had it been clocked, lasted exactly twenty-two and one-half minutes.

* * * *

AFTER:

He scurried home to his apartment, constantly looking in his rear view mirror, expecting sirens as he drove. He failed to consider any havoc he might have left behind him.

"That was too close!" Gus said, talking to himself. He sat down at his desk. "Too close. They know, but how could they know that much about me?" He rubbed his head back and forth. "I left no trail, I covered up everything." His imaginings focused only on the football game, and Kennedy's assassination, where everything was the quarterback's fault.

He even dropped his lawsuit against the bank for taking his mother's money, because he didn't want to give out his new address. He only gave Buddy his phone number, so he wouldn't get suspicious.

Then that witch mentioned his numbers...his sacred numbers, so...he showed her... he burned the list. He panicked for a moment, tensed, forgetting he had made copies. His blubbery shoulders relaxed a bit only after he spied the original in its protective cover on the desk.

Rubbing his head, his fat stubby fingers going back and forth in frustration, he tried recalling the afternoon.

Burning the list had been one of his main ideas, his show of power so to speak. But later...not today...later, down the road. He wanted his revenge, but he expected more time to play with them.

"It's all their fault," he wailed. "That crazy school teacher and that witch!" A sob escaped him. "Ruined!" A tear rolled out of one hard dark eye, coursing down a reddish blue cheek. "My sacred numbers, ...and my great word!"

His gaze lingered on the piles on his desk. All of the plans for the reunion hadn't been done yet, and he wanted it to be done. The band selected, decorations ordered and paid for. Then he could squash it like a melon. He wanted to be a mouse and see their faces, the chumps, and hear their words..the eleven's depended on this committee.. but he'd show them.

Picking up the list, Gus became somewhat wistful, thinking about his beautiful plan, when he heard sirens. Loud, menacing shrieks coming down his block. His heart leaped in his chest, leaving him breathless, unable to move. FBI, he thought immediately. His plan, his mind screamed, Kennedy was killed for his plan!"

Huddled over his desk, his arms trying to encompass everything on his desk, he waited, heart thudding painfully in his chest, waiting for the banging on the door to begin.

To his utter confusion the sirens moved on, the wailing sound getting fainter until his grasp on the desk slowly began to relax. He shook his head trying to ease the pressure that had built up. Gradually he began to think of the changes he would now have to make, the necessary alterations to his plan.

* * * *

Two weeks before Christmas, 1995, strange envelopes began arriving at the homes of the 1946 Spinning High alumni.

With the Post Office in it's usual holiday turmoil, they were delivered along with Christmas cards, the usual catalogs and scads of throw-away mail.

Some were tossed out, thinking they were merely advertisements. But the curious noted the strange numbers, above and below their addresses. In the upper left-hand corner was S.H.S. 46.

There was no return address on the majority of letters sent out, only the numbers 11.22.63, or its variation. The address itself had letters and numbers crossed out, underlined or with unusual spacing.

The brief letter inside was even more curious.

* * * *

Martha was sorting through the mail, laying the Christmas cards off to one side. A letter addressed to Leon caught her attention. "Leon," she called from the kitchen. "Could you come here please."

Leon loved his new recliner, Martha's Christmas present, given to him early simply because she didn't know what to do with it. He hated the early part, preferring it on Christmas day. Reluctantly he got up and shuffled into the kitchen.

"Boy, I sure like that chair, Martha. In fact, I love that chair!" But being Leon, he couldn't let it rest there. "What else are you getting me, something neat, right?" Feeling magnanimous towards Martha, even though she did screw up, he gave her shoulder a loving squeeze. "What's up?"

"Look at this," she said sliding the envelope towards him, as he sat down across from her at the table.

He scanned it slowly trying to figure out what it was all about. "What's this?" he said looking at his name and address underlined with some letters crossed out.

At first the 9 5 2 5 meant nothing, typed above his name, until he looked at the upper left-hand corner, where S.H.S.46., was typed.

It took him a moment, but then he exclaimed, "Jesus! I thought we were all through with this!" He flipped the envelope over. Numbers. He had no idea what they meant. He flipped it back. The 16.32.11. under S.H.S. 46., puzzled him.

He stared so long at the front of the envelope that Martha, bursting with curiosity, had to ask. "Goodness Leon, aren't you going to open it?"

"Oh, yeah, sure," he said absently reaching for the letter opener Martha was extending him. He pulled out one lone 8"x11" sheet of paper hesitantly, holding it by one corner as if it would bite him. Unfolding it, he started to read, pushing himself up from the table.

"Jesus H. Christ!" he exploded. "That son of a bitch!"

Martha quickly got up and moved over to read over his shoulder. "What? What is it Leon?" But Leon was waving it around in the air and she had a difficult time. "Leon, for goodness sakes, what is it?"

With a heavy sigh, he handed it to Martha. "It's from Gus, that son of a bitch. Look what he's done."

* * * *

Maxie opened the door to Jake. "Come on in honey," she said stepping out of the way as he entered. She reached up for his kiss, then quickly closed the door against the cold following him into the front room. The fire burning in the fireplace along with the lights on the Christmas tree, made a cozy setting. He lay his jacket on a chair before sitting down across from her on the couch.

Jake had been carrying his letter from Gus. Maxie's lay open on the coffee table in front of them. "This is just unbelievable, isn't it?" asked Jake holding her letter up.

"I'm so glad you called about it. I threw it away with a bunch of junk and I would have missed it for sure," Maxie smiled at him. "I could hardly believe that he'd go to such lengths."

Jake shook his head. "Devious, just plain devious."

"I talked to Mildred after you called but she hadn't gotten her mail yet. She said she would call me back."

Jake picked up Maxie's letter. Comparing it with his it seemed to be the same until he looked at the envelope. "Look at this," he said.

Maxie moved close to him. "What?"

"Look under S.H.S., up in the corner." He put the envelopes together. "See these numbers, they're different." Jake's read, 36.12.12. Maxie's read, 63.12.21.

"I wonder what it means?" she said looking at Jake. "Strange. But look at those numbers above and below my name. The 0.4.6 after my name has to mean 1946, that's obvious." She looked at Jake's envelope. "Those numbers at least seem to be the same," she said.

They pondered over the numbers until the ringing of the phone interrupted them.

Answering it, Maxie held her hand over the phone. "It's Mildred," she said to Jake. Removing her hand she asked, "Have you read it?" She listened, nodding. "Jake's here with me, we were going over those numbers." She nodded again. "Yes, I agree, that letter is terrible, yes, he's a terrible man."

Putting her hand over the phone again she whispered to Jake, "She's fit to be tied."

Turning back to the phone, she asked, "Have you got a lot of numbers on the front and back of you're envelope?" She nodded her head so that Jake could follow. "He really wants everyone to believe that, doesn't he?"

Jake was motioning to her. "Just a minute Millie, Jake wants me to ask you something." He was pointing to the numbers up on the left-hand corner. "Oh, do you have numbers under the return address part?" She listened. "632112?" she repeated. "Wait a minute, Mil, Jake wants to talk to you."

"Hi Millie. Maxie just read those numbers all together. Is that the way they were typed?" He listened, a frown crossing his forehead. "No dots in between the numbers? Hmmmm." He started to hand the phone back to Maxie, and then spoke into it again. "Bye, Millie, see you," he said and hung up the phone.

* * * *

Mildred was holding the phone to her ear. "Goodbye, Jake, does Maxie"... The line had gone dead. He had hung up..."Well, she said.

"Honestly Ma, some people really have bad manners," she said hanging up the phone. She looked down at the envelope in her hand. "Look at this Ma." She reached over and handed it to Bella. She really wanted to talk some more about it, to go over it bit by bit, dissect it. She looked at the offensive letter in her hand, rereading it.

Sitting down she removed one shoe, holding it in her hand while still reading. Bella watched closely, waiting for Mildred to put the shoe down, bringing back fond memories.

She thought of her long departed husband Dushan. He would always go to bed early since he had to get up at the crack of dawn. Following later, she would creep into the bedroom, trying not to make any noise so as not to waken him.

Taking off her shoes, she would be so busy watching him she would forget and drop the first shoe with a loud thud. Carefully she would lay the second shoe very quietly on the floor, and go about the business of getting ready for bed.

Invariably, after a few minutes or so she would hear, "Bella, for God's sake, drop the other shoe!"

Bella continued to watch Mildred, still holding her shoe, either deep in thought about the letter, or drifting again. She worried it was the latter, and said in her reedy little voice, "Millerd, for God's sake, the shoe, drop the shoe!"

Having heard that story many, many times, Mildred started to laugh. She had not been having an episode, she was just trying to understand why that vile man did what he did. "It's okay Ma," she laughed dropping the shoe. She saw Bella's concerned face and said, "I'd better call Janet."

* * * *

"You're sure it was from Gus? Janet asked Mildred. The mere thought of it filled her with such excitement, causing her heart to beat wildly. "No, I haven't seen anything like that," she said somewhat breathless. "But then Andy opens all the mail here, so I'll have to check with him." She wanted desperately to hang up and run immediately to Andy's den, but checked herself.

"How have you been Mildred?" She barely listened to her friend's responses. Putting her hand to her chest, she interrupted Mildred, feeling she just had to get to that letter.

"Mildred dear, take good care of yourself, tell you're mother hello for me and Merry Christmas to you both. See you soon. "Bye," she said in a rush, leaving Mildred with a dead phone plastered to her ear.

She barely hung up and she was off racing for Andy's den. Opening the door without knocking was sure to upset the

Godman. Hardly noticing the surprised anger on her husband's face, she rushed in.

"Andy," she said breathlessly, "I believe a letter came for me from the Reunion committee. Have you seen it?" In her eagerness she started to move the mail around on his desk, until Andrew grabbed her wrist.

"Stop that!" he said angrily.

"Well tell me, have you seen it?" she demanded, glaring back at him.

"No, I have not!" He stood to face her across the desk. "And, do not talk to me in that tone of voice!" he added.

Forgetting momentarily that she had come in for the letter, she replied, "How do like it?" enjoying the reversed roles.

Andrew puffed himself up, his usual posture when confronted. "I don't!"

She did not back down, but remembering what she was there for, decided she only wanted to get her letter.

"Andy just give me my letter, and I'll get out of here." She noticed him glance down at his wastebasket and she lunged for it, getting it before he could.

He started to grab the basket out of her hand. "Don't." she said fiercely, making him retreat. Looking down she saw a corner of an envelope that had S.H.S. 46., and plucked it out. A glance told her it was for her.

"How dare you decide to throw my mail away!" she said in a tone that made Andrew shrink.

The woman before him, he saw, could no longer be dominated. "I really thought it was junk mail," he said lamely.

Janet walked out of the room, slamming the door behind her. She clutched the letter. It was for her, and it was from Gus.

✳ ✳ ✳ ✳

It was nearing Christmas, a time for festivities, and Buddy and Dee's usual Christmas party. But not this year thanks to Gus. Repairs were still going on, almost two months after the fire.

155

The family room had been completely gutted. The den with Buddy's desk, his pride and joy, ruined by smoke and water damage, as were the other rooms. The only room to survive, practically in tact, was the laundry room.

The experience at first, so demented them, they were beyond anger. Feeling adrift and homeless, they moved in with their daughter, DiDi, becoming almost humble.

Their daughter did not fancy the intrusion, after all she was her mother's daughter, and Dee especially, felt it most strongly. Buddy, unable to bear the constant bickering between the two, found excuses to leave the house whenever he could.

Gone was the toupee. Buddy had suffered minor burns on his head and could not wear anything, even a hat, for the first couple of weeks.

At first, he was mortified. But he began to notice how comfortable he was, outside of the burns. No more checking to see if it was on straight, or if it blended. He always felt self-conscious at anybody looking down on top of his head, which was almost always, given his height. And best of all, gone was the heat that radiated under it, especially when he was upset.

He visited his home almost daily. At first none of the old neighbors recognized him, and tried to hide it when they did. He became accustomed to the stares and the asides, and then they became accustomed to him.

The house looked bleak. It had been stripped down practically to its shell in places. Tarps and plastics covered much of it to keep the seasonal rains out.

It was hard for Buddy to see it that way. How different it had been when they were first building it. Each step had been a birth to them.

Now he remembered the piles of debris. The death of the house, he thought. Dee had only come once, but collapsed, sobbing in his arms. He had to get her away quickly. She could not even bear to talk of it for the first month. It was Buddy, who went inside to collect clothing, jewelry and important papers, anything that hadn't been ruined.

Now thank goodness, he could see she was starting to make plans. She talked of her new home. She still would not go near it, just started looking at wallpaper and samples of material. Asking always, "Is this fire retardant?"

On this particular day, Buddy's step was lighter. He had just left the house, and things were starting to shape up a bit more. The contractor told him they should be in by February.

He decided to stop at the Post Office for their mail. The cards, along with the good news, would help cheer up Dee.

Dee had just had another tiff with DiDi, and was in a foul mood. She hoped Buddy would bring home some good news for a change, although she wasn't sure if she would be able to recognize good news. She just wanted to get out of the rotten situation she was in.

She was tired of DiDi's suggestions, tired of being told to get out and do things. She grabbed a bag of chips and went to sulk in front of the TV.

My God, she thought, all she had said to her daughter was, "Why can't they cook a decent meal for a change?" DiDi as usual hit the roof. Pizza, tacos, chicken. Take-outs, that's all they ever ate. DiDi didn't cook, and her husband Stu didn't seem to mind.

I offered to cook, what's wrong with that? she fumed, going over the argument. "No, you're our guests," her daughter had said. Baloney! She just doesn't like food that's good for her or anybody else. Just look at her and Stu. Fat!

Trouble was, she and Buddy were getting used to it, and even liked the damned take-outs. But she was getting fat and stopped weighing herself after the first five pounds. It was just too depressing.

Dee was always hungry now, and she had to admit, the food was comforting. She never used to eat like this. She remembered. All those aerobics classes, the running and swimming, eating mostly vegetables.

Even Buddy had put on weight. Without his toupee, his face looked rounder, and a hell of a lot older.

It was all going to hell. Gone, everything was gone. All their good habits shot to hell, and she knew it would take more strength than she had, to get them back. She looked like hell, and she really didn't care. She hadn't had a decent manicure or pedicure in months. Gray hair was popping out all over the place. Everything was too much trouble, too much effort. She was either crying or eating.

She sniffed, feeling tears start to well up. "It's all that crazy man Gus's fault! Everything!" She spoke directly to Erica Kane, of All My Children. "God! I wish I had never thought of that stupid reunion!" she lamented, chewing furiously on another chip.

Even the enthusiasm for the house was put on for Buddy's benefit. She could care less and wasn't even sure if she could ever be comfortable there again. Just going through the motions of picking out colors and wallpaper overwhelmed her. All her beautiful decorations had gone up in smoke, and she wasn't sure she could ever come up with anything as wonderful.

I've blown the wad, she told herself. She thought of all the frenzied shopping and picking out, co-ordinating colors, and all those people she dealt with so easily then. But now the whole idea was crushing.

"I just don't want to do that anymore, period!" she told Erica Kane.

The pain behind her eyes was starting up again, and her shoulders hurt. Maybe I'll just go lay down again, she thought, longing for the seclusion of her borrowed bed, and comfy comforter. At least DiDi didn't scrimp on the bedding, and for that one thing, she was grateful.

On her way to the bedroom she heard Buddy come in. "Hell's bell's," she whispered and reluctantly turned to go hear what he had to say. He would just come and get her anyway. She sighed, nobody left her alone.

Buddy looked up when she came shuffling into the room. He was worried, he'd never seen her so depressed. Dee was a fighter he told himself. Granted, she could be a royal pain in the ass, but at least that was better than this, he thought.

"Look honey," he said holding up the mail. "Lot's of cards." She barely acknowledged it. "You know," he continued, "we're going to have to get busy and send cards out." Dee's shoulders slumped. "Oh you know what?" he pressed on, sounding more cheerful than he felt. "Denton said..."

"Who?" she asked.

"Denton, the contractor, you know," he said watching for recognition. She finally nodded. "Anyway, he said the house would probably be ready in February. How about that?"

He got a wan smile for his effort.

Putting his head close to hers, he said quietly, "You know I can hardly wait to get away from here too, and DiDi."

He was expecting at least a smile for that little tid-bit. Nothing.

"Do you want to look at the mail?" He said resigning himself to another dreary day. He laid the bundle down on the coffee table in the family room. Dragging her feet, Dee joined him on the couch.

"Let's see what we have here," he said shuffling through, picking out the cards and handing them to her. "You open these, okay?"

As she listlessly started in on the pile, his eyes fell on an envelope that at first just looked strange, sloppy with letters crossed out. Looking to see who it was from, he noticed S.H.S. 46. Quickly he picked it up, checking to see if Dee had seen it too. Relieved, he saw that she was slowly reading a card, so he had a chance to look the envelope over. What the hell are all these numbers for, he wondered, knowing immediately it was from Gus. His heart began to thud in his chest as he ripped it open.

Getting up from the couch, he walked over to the window, as if he needed more light. He let out an involuntary gasp as he read:

Dear Spinning High Graduates of 1946,

The time for our 50th class reunion is almost upon us. We know you have been looking forward to a glorious party, as you have every right to.

The money that was left over from the last reunion, $700.00 to be exact, has been paid out for a gathering place.

But then we started thinking. This is a lot of work. Why do we have to do it all while you eleven's just sit on you're asses expecting it.

Well by the time we thought of canceling it, we couldn't get the money back, and that was a damn shame. We thought we could at least split it or have a good time with it ourselves.

You're probably thinking you don't need us, you can get your own committee together. But you see...you don't have the list...and you never will. It's been burned.

Maybe, if you ask real nice, another class will let you join them. Of course it won't be the same, it won't be the Class of 1946 having their very own 50th reunion.

It only happens once in a lifetime folks, and you're going to miss it. WHAT A SHAME...

Sincerely,

The names of all the committee members were listed, except of course...Gus's.

* * * *

160

EPILOGUE:

In mid June 1996, the huge banquet room of a popular hotel, lay quiet and dark. However, a small private room off to the side, was alive with music and laughter, even though it was mid-week.

The centerpiece on the elegantly appointed large round table was an arrangement of summer blooms, a contribution from Janet's prolific garden. Rising up from the center, the number 50 in glittering cardboard, picked up the faceted lights from a small revolving mirrored ball. The latter requested and furnished by Dee.

Slim ribbon streamers cascaded from the arrangement, with the printed words, SPINNING HIGH, CLASS OF '46, in small black block letters.

The table was set for nine, with one place still empty.

"I do hope Mildred remembered," said Janet looking at her watch. It read 7:30 P.M. Her wavy white hair beautifully framed her full tan face. She had no fear of the sun and sucked it up as if she were a sponge. The warnings were for other people. The aquamarine floor length chiffon gown was a superb color choice, enhancing her tan even more.

"I called her just before we left, to remind her of the time," she said, concern sounding in her voice.

"Yes, she certainly did," agreed Andrew, looking stiff and stuffed in his black suit. "We even offered to pick her up, too, but she told Janet she wanted to drive in case she had to get home to her Mother, for some reason." He sounded like he had just given a sermon, and began to fidget under Janet's steady gaze.

"Thank you Andrew, I'm sure we all appreciate you're confirmation." It caused Andrew to look down, his face flushed.

All his apologies to Janet, for everything, were not working as well as he expected. He did not understand her new independent nature, but realized it had something to do with that letter she had gotten before Christmas.

Glimpses of the new Janet unsettled him even more when he was left to fend for himself at least once a week, while she went off somewhere for several hours. He knew he dare not ask where.

"I hope nothing's happened to her," said a worried Maxie. She turned to her husband. "Jake, maybe we should have insisted she come with us."

"She's only a half hour late, sweetheart," Jake said patting her hand. "Let's give her a little more time."

He loved looking at her. She had such style. The gray-green jacket, his favorite color on her, with the long slim skirt was elegantly simple. The classic silver and black earrings and bracelet were her only adornments, except of course for her new wedding band.

Leon, in his new white dinner jacket was beaming. He was so glad Buddy had insisted they have their own reunion party. Lord knows, he didn't want anymore to do with this whole thing, but after what they had all been through, especially Buddy and Dee, he couldn't turn him down. Besides, he didn't want Gus to win.

Ms. Keller, the co-ordinator they had worked with months before, listened quietly to Buddy and Leon's story of mayhem and deception by one of the members, and commiserated with them.

All of the weekends were booked at least a year in advance, as they well knew, but she managed to find one day mid-week for them to hold their private celebration. Lord knows the committee did discuss it, and maybe they should have tried to incorporate the whole class somehow, but they didn't have a clue where to begin again or have the heart to even try.

"This is so nice, isn't it?" Leon asked, looking around the table. "I want to make a toast," he said standing up. He looked down at Martha, his eyes sincere, then at the others as cascades of tiny light squares danced over them.

"Small as it is, I think this is going to be one of our best reunions...ever!" He raised his glass, then sat down, pleased with himself.

But it was short-lived, thanks to Dee.

"You know Leon, maybe you should have waited until Mildred got here. After all, we don't know what's happened to her, do we?" she said ever so sweetly, enjoying Leon's fading smile, until Buddy kicked her nearest size four's under the table.

Also under the table, Martha was squeezing Leon's arm after his muttered, "Shit, she's doing it again." and had to apply a little more pressure, until he took a deep breath, trying to relax.

Buddy smiling along with everyone else, until Dee's unnecessary remark, felt betrayed by her behavior. Things had gotten off to a nice start and he saw no need for anymore nastiness. After all, they all had enough of that to last the rest of their lives.

Dee had promised Buddy they would have fun and leave all the bitterness behind them. As if remembering her promise, she gave Buddy a look of apology before turning away, but none to Leon.

Mollified-somewhat, Buddy gave her a sideways glance, noticing how pretty she looked. Gone, were the bony angles of her face and shoulders that always gave her that ferret look of determination. He marveled at the soft plumpness of her, swathed in bold flowered chiffon, with an abundance of ruffles at the neck and sleeve. Large colorful flowered shaped earrings covered her ears, and jewelry dangled around her neck and wrists. Rings of every size and color cut into her pudgy fingers. She did tone down her make-up to only two shades of eyeshadow, and less eyeliner.

Dee belonged to that old school that if a little bit is good, then a whole lot is better. And Buddy agreed, praising her choices, complimenting her on everything she wore.

Dee was finally comfortable with herself. She had not even tried to shed the twenty or so pounds she had gained, able at last to show some compassion towards her overweight daughter.

Dee and DiDi became closer, since Dee no longer competed for DiDi's era, realizing she had her own all along.

Buddy's tux, made for his new rounder plumper frame, fit nicely. He finally felt grown up, no longer needing the driving

163

assurances of looking young. He accepted the fact he would never be taller, his hair was gone and he and Dee were really senior citizens.

They even began to accept the perks of their station and accepted the five or ten percent discount handed out to seniors by many establishments.

His glistening round face with his nearly bald head picked up the facets of light from the mirrored ball. It rolled across all of them sitting at the table and he was pleased to see that there were no objections this time to Dee's idea. He heard greetings called out, interrupting his thoughts. Mildred had finally arrived and he let out a long sigh of relief.

"Hi everyone!" came a cheerful greeting from Mildred, looking around the formally attired group. "Don't you all look wonderful!" she exclaimed. "Dee, I love your hair," she called out, causing Dee to dimple and touch her beautifully coifed gray hair.

Standing over Maxie and Jake, she leaned down, embracing them both. "Congratulations you two, you're absolutely glowing!"

She had been to their small wedding in February, as had the rest of the committee, and the thrill of that day seemed to linger surprisingly, in her depleted memory.

"I'm just so happy for you both," she said. After giving them each a peck on the cheek, she sat down in the empty chair that had been waiting for her.

"Now we can finally get this party going," smiled Leon, relief flooding him. Worry had begun to gnaw at him that he put a jinx on Mildred, after he made that toast. Dee's remark as usual, stung. "By the way Millie, is everything okay?"

They all wanted to ask that question, but didn't know how to approach it, thankful for Leon, who didn't have that problem.

"Well Leon," she started. "Would you believe I started out driving, heading for here, I guess, when I forgot where I was going." She no longer tried to hide her problem from them since the fire. Maxie and Janet had told her what happened, the way she acted that day. At first she tried to deny it, but what good did it do, they already knew.

She looked around at their dear faces, hanging on her every word. "I actually had to pull into a parking lot and sit there, waiting for it to come back to me. I did have a clue however," she continued. "I was wearing an evening gown."

"Then what happened?" asked Dee, leaning forward in her chair. The other's waited.

"Well," she paused. "I kept asking myself, now Mildred," and she laughed. A wonderful high laugh, not quiet a cackle yet, but close.

The others around the table loosened up, grinning back at her.

Mildred began again. "I kept asking myself, now Mildred where in the world could you be going, dressed like this?" She was definitely enjoying herself, and so was her audience.

"I didn't have any other clue mind you, until I turned on the overhead light since the daylight was fading, and then I saw the note.

"So?" said Maxie, anxious for her to go on.

Mildred laughed. "It told me to come here!"

Maxie burst into laughter. Dear, dear Millie, she just loved her. All around her was laughter. She looked across the table at Dee.   Her head was thrown back and she was laughing uproariously.

Martha, unsure at first, wondering how much she was supposed to know, since Leon told her everything, decided it was all right to laugh. Andrew in total ignorance, not sure what to make of any of it could only smile stiffly, checking to see if Janet approved.

Everyone, was touching someone else, in wonderful comradery. Maxie felt Jake's arm go around her, hugging her close and nuzzling her neck. She was so proud of her husband. Still tan from their cruise, he looked so handsome in his white dinner jacket. His wispy white hair, like a halo, added to his rugged good looks, charming her right down to her toes.

"Have I missed anything?" Mildred asked when they settled down, causing them to begin laughing all over again at her choice of words. Mildred joined right in.

Poor Janet was laughing so hard, she had to keep her legs tightly together, hoping she wasn't overflowing.

"You heard we sold the house, didn't you?" Buddy asked when things quieted down again.

"I believe Janet mentioned it, but she didn't know all the details," Mildred answered, not sure if maybe she had forgotten.

"Yes, we fixed it all up, that is we had it rebuilt as you know," Buddy replied. "It looked great too," he added almost longingly.

"I wasn't about to go into all that decorating stuff again," Dee chimed in. "We figured, let whoever buys it, do what they want with it." A slight frown crossed her forehead. "We thought for sure it would take forever to sell, you know, without my touches so to speak. But it was snapped up, sold in a day."

The other five-committee members, to a person, all had their own thoughts on that remark, and couldn't say a word. Even Leon let it pass.

"We found the dearest condo, not too far actually from the house," said Dee, showing her deepest dimples.

"And it's right next to a golf course," gloated Buddy. "I've always wanted to play, so now I will."

Maxie couldn't stand it, she had to know. "What did you decide on, you know?" She didn't want to be too obvious, and Dee was looking at her so strangely, she blurted out, "How are you decorating it Dee?" She felt Jake gently squeeze her arm, waiting for the pinch. He just squeezed.

"Oh that! I didn't, we hired a decorator," Dee said matter-of-factly. "It's all in very early American, antiques and all that old stuff. Kinda plain." She patted her hair. "It's going to take some getting used to, I think."

The squeeze turned into a slight pinch and Maxie had to look away from Dee.

Off to the side, Jeezer, newly graduated, was putting the next old record on the turntable he had set up. It happened to be,

"Smoke Gets in Your Eyes," just one of the records from Jake's collection.

He looked a little stunned at the music he was playing for them, a far, far cry from the heavy metal he was used to. But, he had offered to do it and was being such a good sport

Maxie wanted to run over and hug him.

His hair, still long, but without a trace of blue, was combed back in a ponytail. He had on a decent pair of black pants and shirt, but his large clunky red and white athletic shoes, seemed to cry out that he would only go so far.

Maxie looked lovingly at him, and his look back was so endearing, her heart melted.

They drank, danced, reminisced about old times, even singing along with the old tunes. Everything was lovely, until Leon mentioned Gus.

They were in the middle of their entree, and it was as if time stood still, different expressions crossing each face, remembering.

"Did anyone happen to see that article about Gus, or Merlin in the paper?" Leon said casually. "There were pictures and everything."

"What about?" Buddy asked cautiously

Janet looked up. She stiffened, waiting.

"Well, it seems our old friend was running around naked, gamboling, they actually used that word, gamboling. Anyway, he was splashing in some fountain in some park."

"Really?" Dee was all ears, hoping to hear that something really, really dreadful happened to him.

"Yeah, and he was spouting all these crazy numbers apparently. Does that ring any bells?" Leon looked around, finally getting the attention he had been craving at the meetings.

"They said the postal inspectors had been looking for him, ever since some of those crazy letters he sent out about the reunion, ended up in the dead letter office. I guess some of our classmates complained, too, who knows?"

"How could they know they were from him?" Jake wanted to know, and didn't want to know, but couldn't help himself.

"It seems," Leon said rather impatiently, since he was on a roll. "It seems on some of them, he actually put his P.O. Box number for the return address. Leon beamed, pausing, waiting for it to sink in. "It was a number, get it?" Leon chuckled. "The son of a bitch out-foxed himself!"

"My goodness," said Mildred.

"Anyway, he's in the loony bin," Leon ended, patting down his jacket pocket, needing a cigar. "Damn!" he muttered wishing now he hadn't let Martha talk him out of bringing one. It would have been a capper.

"You said pictures, what pictures?" Buddy asked.

"You know head shot, and the one where they're carting him off." Leon picked up the fork he had laid down and speared a small potato. "Couldn't happen to a nicer fella!" he said with his mouth full.

Janet was looking at her plate. She picked up her knife and slowly started to cut a small small piece from the chicken breast, focusing on the job at hand, tuning out the comments.

Janet desperately wanted to say something, but also didn't want to spoil the evening, knowing how they all felt. Well, she knew, and maybe who knows, with the proper medication, he might even be nice to her some day.

She chewed slowly, thinking about tomorrow and what she would take him. A small pound cake she decided.

Gus loved pound cake.

ABOUT THE AUTHOR

Born in Akron, Ohio, I moved with my parents to California in my teens. I met my husband Wil at Oakland's Fremont High School, graduating together in 1946. We have since shared many class reunions through the years, even working on a few committees.

Shortly after attending our very successful 50th highschool class reunion where Wil and I helped out on the committee, I started to write this book. The group of friends we worked with was such a pleasurable experience, that the thought of everything going wrong seemed like a provocative idea for a story.

This was my first attempt at a novel, quite a departure from the sweet simple short stories in rhyme for children that I love to write.